D1298903

The Political Economy of Education

The CESifo Book Series
Hans-Werner Sinn, editor

The Political Economy of Education: Implications for Growth and Inequality, Mark Gradstein, Moshe Justman, and Volker Meier (2005)

The Decline of the Welfare State: Demographics and Globalization, Assaf Razin and Efraim Sadka, in cooperation with Chang Woon (2005)

The Political Economy of Education

Implications for Growth and Inequality

Mark Gradstein, Moshe Justman, and Volker Meier

CESifo Book Series

The MIT Press
Cambridge, Massachusetts
London, England

© 2005 Massachusetts Institute of Technology

All rights reserved. No part of this book may be reproduced in any form by any electronic or mechanical means (including photocopying, recording, or information storage and retrieval) without permission in writing from the publisher.

This book was set in Palatino on 3B2 by Asco Typesetters, Hong Kong and was printed and bound in the United States of America.

Library of Congress Cataloging-in-Publication Data

Gradstein, Mark.
 The political economy of education : implications for growth and inequality / Mark Gradstein, Moshe Justman, Volker Meier.
    p.   cm. — (CESifo book series)
 Includes bibliographical references and index.
 ISBN 0-262-07256-4 (hc. : alk. paper)
 1. Education—Economic aspects. 2. Education and state. 3. Educational equalization.
4. Human capital. I. Justman, M. II. Meier, Volker, 1966– III. Title. IV. Series.
 LC65.G73   2004
 338.4'337—dc22   2004040293

10 9 8 7 6 5 4 3 2 1

Contents

Series Foreword

This volume is part of the CESifo Book series. Each book in the series aims to cover a topical policy issue in economics. The monographs reflect the research agenda of the Ifo Institute for Economic Research, and they are typically "tandem projects," where internationally renowned economists from the CESifo network cooperate with Ifo researchers. The monographs have been anonymously refereed and revised after being presented and discussed at several workshops hosted by the Ifo Institute.

Preface

The economic organization of education has changed markedly over the past century and a half. Long gone are the miserable, gloomy schools captured so vividly in the novels of Charles Dickens and Charlotte Brontë and the detached, impractical education of the upper classes in the Victorian era. In all advanced industrialized countries today, education is widely recognized as a key to material well-being, both personal and communal, that the state is responsible for supplying in reasonable quality to all school-age children. It is expected to ensure that the young acquire the skills they need to lead an economically productive life and that the national economy is able to compete with other national economies in the global marketplace. Individuals or nations that fail to acquire the education they need must fall behind; in the words of H. G. Wells, "Human history becomes more and more a race between education and catastrophe."

The dominant role that the state plays today in the financing, regulation, and provision of education implies that many of the issues that shape education are resolved through political mechanisms interacting with the individual decisions of households. Parents retain some degree of choice—between public and private education, between different schooling options within the public system—but it is invariably the public sector that plays the leading role in education. This role must be constantly reassessed in light of changing circumstances and changing mores. Changing views on income inequality and social mobility bear on the extent of local involvement in school funding and administration, as well as on public support of private schools. Views on minority rights and the relative advantages of diversity versus homogeneity affect the degree of multiculturalism and religious education that the public education system will accommodate, both internally and in funding private alternatives to public schooling. The relative success and failure of different types of schools give rise to new initiatives aimed at applying successful methods to less successful schools.

These issues require conceptual tools if their implications are to be fully understood, and much progress has been achieved in recent years in developing such tools. This volume offers an overview of these conceptual underpinnings, showing how analytical models can be applied to shed light on central policy issues. It reflects our preference for simpler models that highlight general principles, offering a toolbox of analytical methods for modeling education policy that can then be applied to analyze a wide spectrum of specific applications. Combining analytical rigor and policy relevance, it is aimed at graduate students and senior undergraduates studying the economics of education and education policy, as well as professional analysts and practitioners of education policy with a taste for theory. Of course, much remains beyond the scope of this book, offering rich scope for further research.

The authors gratefully acknowledge the support of CESifo—the international platform of the University of Munich's Center for Economic Studies (CES) and the Ifo Institute for Economic Research—and of Hans-Werner Sinn, who first suggested the project to us. Mark Gradstein and Moshe Justman developed the plan of the book and are jointly responsible for its contents. Volker Meier joined the project midway and contributed to chapters 2 and 6. Parts of this book were presented, as work in progress, at various workshops and seminars, including graduate workshops at Ben Gurion University and at CESifo seminars in Munich. The comments and suggestions we received there were instrumental for the book's evolution, as were the very useful comments of two anonymous reviewers and of Ludger Woessmann, to all of whom we are grateful. Mark Gradstein acknowledges the hospitality of the Research Department at the World Bank during the time the manuscript was finalized.

The Political Economy of Education

1   Introduction

But I am persuaded that in many cases good reasons might be given, why a nation is more polite and learned than any of its neighbors. At least, this is so curious a subject that it were a pity to abandon it entirely.

—David Hume, "Of the Rise and the Progress of the Arts and Sciences" (1742)

In contemporary societies, the education of the young is overwhelmingly a public responsibility. It is invariably compulsory, fully or heavily subsidized, and either publicly provided by employees of the state or closely regulated with regard to attendance, curriculum, teaching staff, physical facilities, class size, and achievement standards. While private education continues to function and offer alternatives or supplements to public schooling, it generally operates in the shadow of larger public systems. This predominant role of the public sector in education is evident in its large share in the funding of elementary and secondary education, which exceeds 90 percent on average in the industrialized countries that comprise the Organization of Economic Cooperation and Development (OECD). In less developed countries, this share is generally lower but is still very substantial. Among OECD countries, these public investments in education account for 13 percent of total government spending, on average, and 6 percent of gross domestic product (GDP).

This is a recent phenomenon in historical perspective. Public involvement in education in preindustrial societies was rare and where it existed was largely limited in scope and almost always motivated by religion. The transformation began in the eighteenth century in western Europe, impelled by a combination of powerful factors. Reformation and Enlightenment, industrialization and urbanization, and the emergence of secular states and democratic forms of government all contributed to the notion that universal public education was a worthy cause with strong moral, social, political, and economic justifications. Adam Smith, Thomas Paine, and John Stuart Mill are among the political economists of the time who gave eloquent expression to a widening recognition that the education of the young was a matter of central public concern for society.

The systems of public education that subsequently evolved are inherently political: they depend on political as well as on market mechanisms to mediate diverse individual preferences regarding the level of public spending on education, the structure of the education system, and the goals it is meant to achieve. These mechanisms of communal decision making are many and varied, ranging from direct democracy in the spirit of the Greek polis of antiquity or the modern kibbutz, to authoritarian regimes in which public opinion has only an indirect effect on the decisions that are reached; from the centralized, largely uniform French education system to the decentralized, heterogeneous structure of education in the United States.

This is the context in which the rich public debate on a wide range of education issues takes place. As education systems expand to meet increasing demand for wider schooling and as the goals of education adapt to changing circumstances and changing mores, there repeatedly arises the need for change and reform of these systems, often raising contradictory demands. Calls for improved governance through tighter control and supervision must be squared with conflicting desires for greater independence of schools to meet specific local needs. Initiatives aimed at improving school performance by fostering a more competitive environment for schools, through vouchers and other means, must be reconciled with concerns that public schools should offer equal opportunity for all.

A theoretical understanding of the political economy of education is necessary for disentangling the complex links between education, growth, and income distribution and for formulating effective policies designed to improve the public financing and provision of education.

Economic Models of Education: What Does Education Do?

Economic theories of education see its value as deriving from one (or more) of the following characterizations—each of which informs a different analytical perspective on the impact of education on economic welfare. Education is variously viewed as

- Building human capital by teaching skills that directly enhance productivity,[1]
- Providing a screening mechanism that identifies ability,[2]
- Building social capital by instilling common norms of behavior,[3] and
- Providing a consumption good that is valued for its own sake.

While most schools address all of these four dimensions, they do so in varying degrees and with different emphases.

Analyses that focus on the role of education in building human capital view it as an investment that yields a return, much like investments in physical capital. This approach emphasizes the role of education as an engine of growth and underlies much of the recent theoretical and empirical analysis of comparative growth rates. It suggests the possibility of positive spillovers that play a key role in formal treatments of endogenous growth and provide a rationale for publicly subsidizing education.

The view that holds education principally as a screening device—helping employers identify the potential productivity of their prospective employees—suggests that the private returns from education may exceed its social returns. When education is a less than perfect screening mechanism, the decisions of less able individuals to pursue schooling generate negative spillovers for others, making them appear less productive. This calls into question the efficiency of publicly subsidizing education; and where public financing is provided for other objectives, it indicates a reason for screening applicants on the basis of their prior academic indicators.[4]

Analyses that focus on the role of education in building social capital emphasize the social returns from education. This rich perspective, which features prominently in the noneconomic literature on public education, emphasizes its advantages for society at large: instilling patriotic values, developing a sense of community, inhibiting criminal and other antisocial behavior, providing a common language and cultural norms that improve the efficiency of communication and economic transactions, and providing young citizens with the tools to become informed, sensible voters. All of these considerations strongly reinforce the case for public involvement not only in financing elementary and high school education but also in regulating its content.

Most economic growth models that address education issues adopt a human-capital approach, describing education—in elementary and high school, on which we focus here—as an investment that parents make on behalf of their children, generally from altruistic motives. This is the approach we adopt in most of our formal analysis, with only chapter 8 devoted to an investigation of the role of education in building social capital.

Why Public Education?

The dominant role of government in education stands in contrast to the absence of an obvious rationale that would explain why it is not generally left to the private sector. Education is not a pure public good in the sense that public goods are defined in economic theory: it is easily excludable (there is no difficulty charging tuition fees), and the marginal cost associated with providing education to an additional child approaches its average cost at modest scales of operation. Moreover, as numerous studies have shown (some of which are reviewed in the following chapter), private returns to education are substantial, often exceeding returns to investment in physical capital, so that one could expect the large majority of the population to acquire their education privately if public education were not available.

In this section, we discuss separately why education should be publicly financed and why it should be publicly administered.

Why Public Financing?

Economic models of education that view it as investment in human capital justify public financing of education on efficiency grounds by referring to the externalities it generates. Indeed, much of the theory of endogenous growth rests on the assumption that such spillover effects exist and are important (Lucas, 1988; Romer, 1986). Romer (1986), Rustichini and Schmitz (1991), and Gradstein and Justman (1997), among others, draw policy implications for providing education subsidies, which follow from the existence of direct production spillovers stemming from individual investments in education. Acemoglu (1996) provides microfoundations for spillover effects of education in production, based on a matching model between firms' investment decisions and individuals' education choices.

Empirical support for this assumption has been somewhat elusive. Existing estimates of the social return to education, though positive, typically fall below private returns (see chapter 3). Presumably, direct production spillovers are relatively more important at the elementary school level, where basic skills are taught—skills that facilitate the communication necessary for all economic activity. However, education also generates other important spillovers that have a less direct effect on growth and may therefore be more difficult to measure. For example, education may decrease the propensity to engage in different kinds of criminal activity. Ehrlich (1975) in an early paper found support for the hypothesis that education and a more equal distribution of income reduce the incidence of crimes against property. More recent evidence to this effect is provided in Lochner and Moretti (2001), who report that social savings associated with crime reduction as a result of high school graduation may amount to as much as one quarter of the private returns to schooling. Additional nonmarket education spillovers are surveyed in Haveman and Wolfe (1984) and Wolfe and Zuvekas (1997). These include the impact of education levels on health-related outcomes such as life expectancy and child mortality, on fertility, on democratization and political rights, on children's education attainment, on environmental quality, and so on.

Historians of education emphasize the role of public schooling in integrating immigrants into the mainstream of society (Good and Teller, 1969). More generally, public schooling can promote social cohesion among disparate social groups and alleviate ethnic tensions by providing a core set of common norms that foster trust and promote interaction among individuals. In the words of Milton Friedman (1962, p. 86),

A stable and democratic society is impossible without a minimum degree of literacy and knowledge on the part of most citizens and without widespread acceptance of some common set of values. Education can contribute to both. In consequence, the gain from education of a child accrues not only to the child or to his parents but also to other members of society. The education of my child contributes to your welfare by promoting a stable and democratic society. It is not feasible to identify the particular individuals (or families) benefited and so to charge for the services rendered.

These social benefits of education and their economic implications are considered more fully in chapter 8.

Preexisting distortions are another possible rationale for public intervention in education. For example, progressive income taxation may cause private returns to schooling to fall below true social returns, implying the need to subsidize schooling as a second-best policy; this perspective is developed in Bovenberg and Jacobs (2001). A related reason is the existence of social "safety nets" that ensure a minimal level of income and public services, irrespective of individual income. These indicate the possibility of moral hazard undermining demand for education: individuals (or their parents, on their behalf) anticipate receiving a helping hand from society and consequently choose to underinvest in schooling. Setting mandatory schooling requirements is one way of addressing this problem, as Bruce and Waldman (1991) have shown.

Imperfection of credit markets is another potentially important source of market failure that is often cited as implying a need for public financing of education. Credit constraints in financing tertiary education may be partially alleviated by providing publicly guaranteed student loans, as is done in the United States. However, this does not apply to K–12 education. The children that would be the direct beneficiaries of such loans are not of an age that allows them to undertake legal obligations, so it is not practically possible to use their future earnings to secure loans to their parents to finance the education of their children. Consequently, absent public financing, poorer parents are credit-constrained in educating their children—their children's ability and motivation notwithstanding.[5]

These considerations emerge from a human-capital view of education, which is predominant in the analysis of the economics of education. The alternative view of education as a screening mechanism can lead to different conclusions. In this view, schooling is perceived not as a way of directly enhancing the potential productivity of an individual but as a means of classifying individuals according to their productivity potential. This view lends much less support for public financing of education on efficiency grounds, as it implies that the decisions of less productive individuals to attend school entail *negative* spillovers for other, more productive individuals, who are thus rendered less easily distinguishable. This carries policy implications that can be very different from those of the human-capital approach. Ultimately, policy choices must rely on empirical estimates of private versus social returns to schooling, which we discuss in chapter 3.

Of course, public financing of education is widely justified on grounds other than efficiency. Education is frequently viewed as a merit good, consumption of which is mandated by the state because individuals may lack the good judgment necessary to act in their own best interest. John Stuart Mill (1848, bk. 5, ch. 11, sec. 8) was an early proponent of this view:

But there are other things, of the worth of which the demand of the market is by no means a test; things of which the utility does not consist in ministering to inclinations, nor in serving the daily uses of life, and the want of which is least felt when the need is greatest.... It will continually happen, on the voluntary system, that, the end not being desired, the means will not be provided at all.... Education, therefore, is one of those things which it is admissible in principle that a government should provide for the people.

With regard to the education of the young, this approach is reinforced because schooling decisions are made by parents on behalf of their children; in making education free and compulsory, the state is acting to safeguard the interests of children whose parents may be unable or unwilling to act in their best interests. If all children are to have the basic opportunities to which they are inherently entitled, government must break the link between the ability to pay and the provision of a basic amount of schooling.[6] Moreover, public financing of uniform education not only promotes equality of opportunity but also can promote income equality in the next generation by effectively redistributing income from rich families to poor families. This may be desirable in its own right and also because it reduces potential political pressures for further redistribution, which reduces both the tax burden and the propensity to engage in violent means of expropriation.

In the United States, for example, where education is decentralized and traditionally has been financed in large measure from local property taxes, legal challenges to the system have argued that letting the quality of a child's education depend on the wealth of the school district in which the child happens to reside violates the "equal protection" clauses of state constitutions. Following the landmark *Serrano v. Priest* decision in 1971, in which the California Supreme Court held that such "wealth discrimination" is unconstitutional, and similar cases in other states, many states have adopted more egalitarian systems of education financing in which state governments are playing an active role in redistributing income from rich to poor school districts.

Efficiency implications of egalitarian educational policies are a subject of some controversy. Maximization of output is achieved by allocating education spending to equalize the marginal return to schooling across individuals. If parental income is strongly correlated with the productivity of schooling and liquidity constraints are mild, uniform public spending on education is a less efficient means of achieving a more equal income distribution than the direct redistribution of income through taxation. Conversely, if the children of poorer parents have a higher marginal return from education, possibly due to the credit constraints alluded to above,[7] then allocating relatively more education resources to the poor than to the rich would promote both equity and efficiency. An important, controversial, empirical issue in this regard is the relative importance of innate abilities in determining economic productivity[8] and the extent to which formal schooling can compensate for a disadvantaged home.

Why Public Provision?

All of the above arguments militate for public financing of education but not necessarily for public provision. Yet in industrialized countries the vast majority of children in elementary and secondary education attend schools that are not only publicly financed but also publicly administered. Thus, in the United States approximately 90 percent of school-age children attend public schools (National Center for Education Statistics, 2000), and similar percentages are observed in other developed countries (OECD, 2001a). The state typically takes full responsibility for school building and maintenance, staffing of teachers, curriculum design, testing scholastic achievement, and so on and requires attendance from the age of five or six through adolescence. Moreover, these features characterize not only countries where the state has traditionally undertaken an active role in the provision of welfare services, such as the Scandinavian countries, but also in societies that emphasize individualistic values, such as the United States.

The prevalence of publicly provided schooling can be rationalized by several arguments, some of which are interrelated. The principle of specific egalitarianism charges the state with the moral responsibility of providing children with a minimal level of basic education. Arguably, a uniform public school system is more likely to achieve this objective than a publicly funded private education system. Publicly provided education has also been widely viewed as an important component in the process of state building. Historically, the emergence of government intervention in schooling in the eighteenth and nineteenth centuries was closely tied to its socializing role, as we show in the following chapter. More recently, publicly provided education has played an important role in efforts to forge new national identities in the multiethnic developing countries that emerged in the second half of the twentieth century. Students of the historical development of public education in the United States as ideologically diverse as Bowles and Gintis (1976) and Friedman (1962) have emphasized the important socializing role it played, which Friedman (p. 96) recognized in presenting the case for school vouchers:

The major problem in the United States in the nineteenth and early twentieth century was not to promote diversity but to create the core of common values essential to a stable society.... Immigrants were flooding the United States ... speaking different languages and observing diverse customs.... The public school had an important function in this task, not least by imposing English as a common language.

This socializing role of education provides a key to understanding the ubiquitous role of the public sector in the provision of primary and high school education: ideological and cultural content are difficult to monitor at arm's length without the direct controls of public administration.[9] Ironically, this militates against using vouchers to finance private schools from public funds—from Friedman's point of view—as such schools may promote cultural divisions and hinder assimilation.

The Scope of the Book

This volume addresses these central issues in the political economy of education through interconnected theoretical frameworks that allow the systematic analysis of these issues within a macroeconomic context. Its main focus is on primary and secondary education (K–12). Additional important channels through which schooling is acquired—such as preschool education, higher education, and on-the-job training—are sufficiently different in their institutional settings and decision-making processes to warrant separate treatments. And its policy-oriented approach dictates the way the arguments are presented. It relies on formal economic reasoning but keeps mathematical material to a minimum (relegating it to appendices where possible) and emphasizes its application to policy issues.

The book begins, in chapter 2, with an overview of historical evidence on the development of public education over time, which is followed in chapter 3 by a review of current econometric evidence on how public education affects and is affected by income levels, income growth, and the distribution of income. This sets the stage for the main body of analysis, which begins with two chapters that lay the theoretical groundwork: chapter 4 develops a basic static model of how political decisions determine education spending and compares pure public and private education in terms of the outcomes they induce, and chapter 5 extends the model dynamically. This allows us to consider income dynamics and intergenerational mobility under public schooling, to compare private and public education in the long run, to consider the structure of popular support for public education, and to examine the links between education and redistributional conflict. This framework is then applied in the last three chapters to three large issues that frame many of the current policy debates on public education. Chapter 6 addresses the political economy of education in a federal context in which there are two levels of government, "central" and "local" (corresponding to state and local financing in the United States) and compares education finance under different regimes of fiscal decentralization. Chapter 7 considers individual choice between public and private schooling, its interaction with residential location and religious preferences, and the use of education vouchers as a means of combining public financing of education with private provision. Chapter 8 focuses on the social dimension of education and its important role as a key element of the "melting pot"—building bridges between new immigrants and the mainstream indigenous culture and promoting cohesion in a culturally diverse society. In all these chapters, a closing section briefly summarizes our main conclusions. Chapter 9 indicates directions for future research.

Historical and Institutional Perspectives

At first, if a child had a father his father taught him, and if he had no father he did not learn at all. . . . At length Joshua ben Gamla came and ordained that teachers of young children should be appointed in each district and each town, and that children should enter school at the age of six or seven.

—Babylonian Talmud, Baba Batra 21:1

In this chapter we present an overview of the historical evolution and institutional structure of public education in different settings—its historical development, summary statistics on the role of the public sector in modern education systems, and brief surveys of four contemporary education systems. It provides some perspectives on contemporary policy issues, which we examine in greater depth in the following chapters.

Historical Evolution of Public Education

Traditionally, society has seen parents as bearing a natural responsibility for the education of their children, though it has often recognized the communal importance of education and intervened to ensure that parents meet their responsibilities in this regard. Plato's *Republic* placed great importance on the education of the guardians of the city,[1] and both the Greek polis and Roman republic required citizens to train their sons in the physical arts, at their own expense, to prepare them for military service. In seeking to aid parents in meeting the biblical injunction to teach their sons to read and understand scripture so that the sacred teachings of the Torah would be remembered and observed, the Judean theocracy, under Roman rule, developed one of the earliest recorded systems of publicly administered education for the general population. The sages regulated curriculum, teacher employment, class size, and disciplinary measures, all of which are discussed in detail in the Talmud.[2] The schools were thus publicly administered, though they were not publicly financed, except for orphans and the children of indigent parents.

The seeds of public education in the modern era can be found in the Protestant Reformation of the sixteenth century. Before the Reformation, most teaching was done by parents at home or through an apprenticeship, with church-affiliated schools devoted to the training of the clergy. The Reformation promoted literacy through education as a means of increasing direct popular access to scripture, thus weakening the monopoly of the clergy on sacred teachings.[3] Compulsory schooling laws were enacted in several places in the seventeenth century, in the German states as well as in Massachusetts and other East Coast colonies. However, these laws were not effectively enforced, the school year was short with many interruptions for work in the fields, and the vast majority of pupils who attended school did so for only a few years (Cubberley, 1919; Good and Teller, 1969).

Greater changes came later, beginning in the eighteenth century. The Enlightenment placed central moral and social value on the development of rational faculties through education.[4] The rulers of the newly forming secular autocracies of Europe sought to establish the roots of their legitimacy, reduce crime, and promote civic virtues through education.[5] And the economic, social, and political forces unleashed by the Industrial Revolution, urbanization, and democratic reform greatly reinforced these trends.

Thus Adam Smith (1976/1776) advocated public education nearly a century before the enactment of compulsory, and later free, education in Britain, primarily on moral grounds. He recognized that the economic efficiency of the pin factory imposed a heavy cost on the soul of the common laborer and saw it as the moral duty of society to rectify this damage through public education:

The man whose whole life is spent in performing a few simple operations ... generally becomes as stupid and ignorant as it is possible for a human creature to become.... Though the state was to derive no advantage from the instruction of the inferior ranks of people, it would still deserve its attention that they should not be altogether uninstructed. (bk. 5, ch. 1, art. 2)

Yet as Adam Smith observed, the state derives considerable advantage from the education of the masses, through which they become "more decent and orderly." Especially when democratic reforms require government to secure broad popular support, it is "of the highest importance that they should not be disposed to judge rashly or capriciously." Similar sentiments were expressed by Thomas Paine (1984/1792, pt. 2, "Ways and Means of Improving the Condition of Europe") in proposing a voucher scheme to finance the education of the poor, so that through their economic advancement they might become better citizens:

Ignorance will be banished from the rising generation, and the number of poor will hereafter become less, because their abilities, by the aid of education, will be greater.... A nation under a well-regulated government should permit none to remain uninstructed. It is monarchical and aristocratical government only that requires ignorance for its support.

The practical beginnings of modern public education can be found in the efforts of the enlightened secular autocratic regimes of Prussia and Austro-Hungary, in the eighteenth century, to establish their legitimacy through the education of the masses. In Prussia, under Frederick William I, schooling was declared to be compulsory in two acts of legislation, in 1717 and 1737, though enforcement was initially lax. The General Civil Code of 1794 established the *Volksschule*, the public elementary school, as an institution of the state, financed mostly from local taxes. It maintained the segregation of Catholic and Protestant schools and was placed under the supervision of the church dioceses and local clergy (Lamberti, 1989).[6]

The creation of a Prussian Ministry of Education and Religious Affairs in 1817 institutionalized the historical link between church and school, while also promoting the professionalization of elementary teaching through teacher-training schools and certification. Religious involvement in the public school system was viewed as furthering the schools' mission as an instrument of social control—establishing the legitimacy of the state in the minds of the general population and forging a sense of national identity—while bringing literacy to the masses. Interconfessional schools were seen as an implicit threat to the social order, except in the eastern regions, where local administrators saw them as a useful vehicle for assimilating the local ethnic Polish population into the German culture. Indeed, the strong involvement of the church hierarchies in public education ensured that public elementary schools enjoyed a near monopoly in Prussia, outnumbering private schools by a ratio of thirty-four to one by 1861. Secondary education also developed in this period, preparing select young men for jobs that required specific skills, particularly in public administration. The outlines of Germany's three-tier secondary education system can be traced back to the late eighteenth and early nineteenth centuries. In 1812, legislation established the *Gymnasium* as a state institution providing nine years of schooling for the elite, and detailed ministerial decrees regulated admissions to the *Gymnasien*, determined curricula, and set the length of the school year and the working hours of teachers (Lundgreen, 1980).[7]

In the decade following German unification, the Bismarck administration initiated a cultural offensive, the *Kulturkampf*, aimed at establishing the sovereignty of the state in education and undermining the influence of the church on state schools, as a concomitant to the political unification of Germany and as part of a wider liberal program of social reform and civic emancipation (Lamberti, 1989). At the initiative of the liberals and the schoolteachers' associations, a series of laws and directives was enacted that sought to establish interconfessional schools as the norm and effectively removed large numbers of parish clergy from administrative and supervisory positions in state schools. There followed massive Catholic demonstrations protesting the changes in the education system, as well as protests from Protestant clergy who feared the merging of confessional schools in cities with small Protestant minorities.

The end result varied from state to state: mixed schools prevailed in Baden and Hesse-Darmstadt, were imposed in the eastern provinces of Prussia as an instrument to suppress Polish nationality, but remained very much the exception in Prussia, where the reforms were largely undone in the 1880s. Confessional schools were confirmed as the normative form of education in Prussia in the school law of 1906, and as late as 1930 well over 90 percent of both Catholic and Protestant children attended schools of their own faith. The strong link between education and religion in Prussia reflected a depth of popular religious sentiment and the importance most people attached to religious instruction as a central pillar of education, as well as the overriding dependence of education on local funding. These factors prevented a liberal Protestant elite from imposing its national priorities on local schools. The *Kulturkampf* galvanized the political organization of Catholic opposition to liberal reform, which joined forces with conservative Protestant elements that came to see the advantage of the confessional structure of the state school system, as it kept religious schools within the public domain and promoted allegiance to the state (Lamberti, 1989).

In France, the centralized education system created by Napoleon in the early nineteenth century survived the Restoration and was subsequently reinforced. As in the German states, it was seen as an important element in creating a single national identity that standardized the French language and furthered the consolidation and dissemination of a uniform national culture. The landmark Loi Guizot of 1833 extended state control over the inspection of schools and the licensing of teachers. By midcentury public schools outnumbered private schools at the elementary level and were almost as numerous as private schools at the secondary level. The Ferry law of 1882 made elementary education free, universal, and compulsory, further increasing the proportion of students enrolled in public schools, and private schools, too, were subjected to state inspection. Education came to reside firmly within the domain of the state, which replaced the Catholic Church in this regard.

At the secondary and tertiary levels, the prestigious and highly competitive *lycées* and *collèges* had a virtual monopoly on training graduates for careers in the civil service. This system was designed to serve the interests of the elite and, as such, restricted social mobility. The ideal of equal opportunity in education came to be articulated only after World War II. The educational reforms of the postwar era enabled children from disadvantaged homes to attend secondary schools, while also promoting technical and vocational training through the creation of *collèges techniques* (Green, 1990; Good and Teller, 1969).

Education in the United States has always been less centralized than in most European countries.[8] Until the midnineteenth century, most elementary education in the United States was publicly operated by local jurisdictions and only partially funded from public sources. The decades before the American Civil War saw the emergence of an egalitarian education reform movement, which spurred increasing involvement in education by the individual states, especially in the industrial North,[9] with the southern states following suit after the Civil War and Reconstruction. In New York, public schools accounted for 82 percent of total enrollment in 1850, and in Massachusetts—the first state to introduce compulsory education, in 1852—89 percent of schoolchildren attended public schools by 1865. Nationwide, public expenditure accounted for 47 percent of total education spending in 1850 and two-thirds in 1870; and in the decades that followed virtually every state adopted full public funding of elementary education (Goldin, 1999).[10]

High enrollment rates generally preceded compulsory attendance laws, which came into effect only after the majority of children were already attending school. Elected local school boards regulated school terms, assigned textbooks, and often appointed teachers, while the states assumed the role of regulating education through the offices of school superintendents charged with overseeing the activities of the local school committees. A common school experience for all was viewed as a key goal of public schools—a goal that grew in importance with the large influx of immigrants around the turn of the twentieth century (Bowles and Gintis, 1976).

The "second transformation" of American education (Goldin, 1998) raised the proportion of high school graduates from 10 percent in 1910 to over 50 percent in 1940, with the most rapid expansion occurring in the non-South regions between 1920 and 1935. The "high school movement" began in the small towns of America's agricultural heartland and was strongest in communities with greater economic, ethnic, and religious homogeneity and greater stability and in agricultural areas where the opportunity cost of schooling was lower than in the manufacturing centers (Goldin and Katz, 1999; Goldin, 1998). The purpose and type of education also changed markedly in this period: before 1910 a high school education was mostly aimed at preparation for college, but the egalitarian high school movement restructured it as a terminal degree aimed at preparing graduates for a growing number of white-collar jobs. Annual returns to secondary school education were as high as 12 percent in 1914 and provided substantial private incentives for high school attendance (Goldin, 1999).[11]

Of course, public education in the United States was not egalitarian for African Americans throughout this period. The process of dismantling racially based segregation in public education began only in 1954, with the U.S. Supreme Court's landmark decision in *Brown v. Board of Education*, which ruled that "separate educational facilities are inherently unequal" and hence stand in contradiction to the Fourteenth Amendment to the Constitution, which declares that "No State … [may] deny to any person within its jurisdiction the equal protection of laws." This began a process of de jure integration of public school systems throughout the country, though de facto integration has proved more elusive. Equal protection clauses in state constitutions have served as the basis for equalizing education financing among school districts in individual states, a process set in motion by the California Supreme Court's *Serrano v. Priest* decision of 1971, which ruled against large disparities in school spending between rich and poor districts and was followed by similar judicial and administrative decisions in other states.

Similar processes of transformation of educational systems from private, community-based systems to public, state-based systems took place in many developing countries in the twentieth century. Although the diverse experiences of the evolution of public schooling in these countries are difficult to summarize briefly, they appear to share some common features. Under colonial rule, much of the education in these countries was provided in the family or through apprenticeships. Formal schooling was predominantly supplied by various missionary organizations and was often fee-paying. Education at an advanced level was frequently geared toward the need to educate a local administrative elite. In ethnically and racially diverse countries, separate schools were established for different ethnolinguistic groups. The postcolonial period of the 1950s and 1960s saw the emergence of public schooling in these countries, the primary aim of which was to provide an adequate level of primary education to the population at large while ensuring uniform linguistic and cultural standards. In many developing countries in Africa and Asia, public education has served as a tool in the process of nation building, in much the same way it did in Europe a hundred years before.

By the 1970s many of these countries had committed themselves to guaranteeing a minimal level of at least four years of primary schooling. In Ghana, for example, primary education became free and compulsory in 1961, in Kenya free primary education was introduced in 1974, and in Nigeria in 1976. The proportion of the student population enrolled in public schools has risen continuously, with private education often placed under state supervision. The growing number of students with elementary schooling created a natural demand for secondary schooling, which expanded as well. Universities, which were essentially nonexistent in many of the developing countries under colonial rule, were also established, and by the 1980s every African country had at least one university; Ghana, the first African nation to gain independence in the postwar period, had three (Babs Fafunwa and Aisuku, 1982).

The Role of the Public Sector in Modern Education

The predominant role of the public sector in education is evident from table 2.1, which presents the share of public funding in elementary and secondary education for a selection of countries. Among the

Table 2.1
Proportion of public funds in primary, secondary, and postsecondary nontertiary education, selected countries, 1998

Country	Percentage	Country	Percentage
OECD		*Other*	
Australia	84.1	Argentina	89.4
Austria	94.8	Chile	68.7
Canada	91.7	Indonesia	81.8
Czech Republic	87.5	Israel	92.8
Denmark	97.9	Jordan	100.0
France	92.7	Peru	61.8
Germany	75.9	Philippines	59.7
Hungary	92.0	Thailand	62.7
Ireland	96.9	Uruguay	93.1
Italy	99.0		
Japan	91.7		
Korea	79.3		
Mexico	86.2		
Netherlands	94.3		
Norway	99.1		
Portugal	99.9		
Spain	89.2		
Sweden	99.8		
Switzerland	88.1		
Turkey	78.2		
United States	90.8		
OECD country mean	90.9		

Source: OECD (2001a), indicator B2.

industrialized countries that comprise the Organization of Economic Cooperation and Development (OECD), the average share exceeds 90 percent. In developing countries, this share is generally lower but is still very substantial. In these countries, where the state continues to expand its role in education, initial efforts are generally directed to guaranteeing universal primary schooling and setting uniform curricula guidelines.

This deep involvement of the state in education is, of course, also reflected in the large proportion of students attending public schools (table 2.2).

Public expenditures on education account for a large fraction of gross domestic product (figure 2.1), nearly 6 percent among OECD

Table 2.2
Public share in education enrollment, 1999

Country	Percentage
Australia	75
Canada	95
France	79
Germany	95
Italy	94
Japan	89
Spain	70
Sweden	98
United Kingdom	65
United States	89

Source: OECD (2001a).

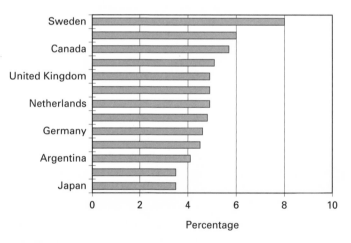

Figure 2.1
Public expenditure on education as a percentage of GDP, 1998
Source: OECD (2001a).

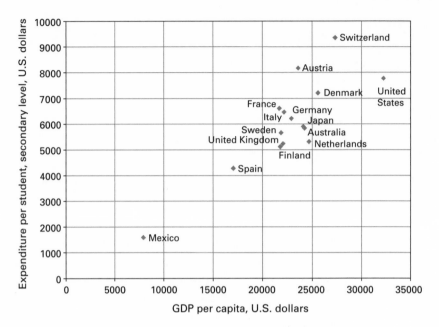

Figure 2.2
GDP per capita and spending per student, 1998
Source: OECD (2001a).

countries; and for a large share of government spending, almost 13 percent among OECD countries. This reflects an increase in funding per pupil to unprecedented levels (figure 2.2). OECD countries spend, on average, almost $4,000 or 19 percent of GDP per capita, per primary student, and around $5,700, or 25 percent of GDP per capita, per secondary student. At the same time, compulsory schooling in most advanced industrial countries has been extended to the ages of sixteen to eighteen.[12]

These common features highlight similarities among modern education systems in many countries, but there are also important differences. Thus in some countries, such as the United States and Denmark, the state delegates much of the responsibility for education to local communities, whereas in others, such as Japan, the control of education is more centralized. These differences are reflected in figure 2.3, which presents data on the fiscal decentralization of education in a sample of countries. Note that in countries with a federal structure, such as the United States and Germany, fiscal responsibility for education typically rests largely with subnational regional authorities (such

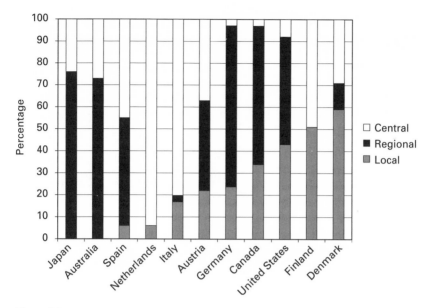

Figure 2.3
Initial sources of public education funding by level of government, 1995
Source: OECD (1998).

as the states in the United States), while in other countries the residual responsibility not delegated to local jurisdictions remains at the national level. Decentralization of education funding is therefore best compared across nations by comparing the share of local spending on education, which ranges from 0 in Australia and Japan, to 59 percent in Denmark.[13]

Another dimension along which education systems differ is the extent in which private schools are eligible for public funds. Some countries, to a far greater extent than others, provide public funding to private schools and intervene in their operation. Figure 2.4 presents evidence on the share of public expenditures on schooling spent on private institutions in selected countries.

Four Education Systems

We conclude this chapter with a brief survey of the structure of the education system in four countries: Germany, the United States, Chile, and New Zealand. While these systems share important common characteristics—notably a strong commitment to free, compulsory

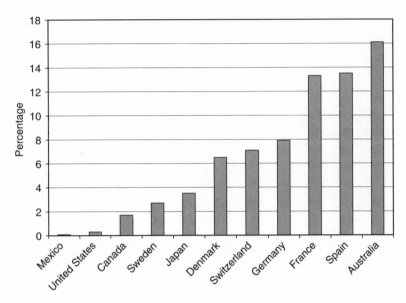

Figure 2.4
Share of K–12 public funds allocated to private schools, 1999
Source: OECD (2002).

schooling that is publicly financed and regulated by government—
they differ in the role that government plays in the direct operation
of schools and in the extent to which the education system is
decentralized.

Germany
Compulsory schooling in Germany begins at age six and continues
over a period of nine to ten years of full-time primary and lower secondary education, which may be followed by up to three years of full-
or part-time additional public schooling (European Commission, 1995).
After four to six years, pupils are streamed into one of three types of
secondary school. Those showing the highest promise are sent to a
Gymnasium, which provides lower and upper secondary schooling,
with a final examination after twelve or thirteen years of schooling;
this final exam is a prerequisite for entering university. Intermediate
achievers are sent to a *Realschule* and are examined after ten years of
schooling, while the lowest achievers attend a *Hauptschule*, which leads
to a final exam after nine or ten years of education. After completing
one of the two lower tracks, pupils may continue their education in
vocational training over a period of two to three additional years. This

stratified system of secondary education exists in all states, but many parents also have the option of sending their children to comprehensive schools where ability tracking may vary. Students in a comprehensive school can, in principle, sit for any of the three main exams. Transferring from one school type to another is also possible within the stratified system.

It is a reflection of the federal structure of Germany that public education is organized and financed primarily at the state level, with the federal government playing a minor role in primary and secondary education.[14] The sixteen states each decide on the aims and methods of instruction in the schools under their jurisdiction, determine their curricula, and set final exams, while maintaining some measure of coordination to ensure that qualifications are roughly comparable. In 1995, about 75 percent of primary and secondary education funding came from regional authorities, with the remaining 25 percent funded by local authorities and nonprofit organizations. Local authority funds are used mostly for school maintenance and administration, while nonprofit organizations, acting on behalf of parent groups, offer supplemental activities that vary with differences in income and preferences across localities. The amount of public money that schools receive is determined by their enrollment, and because the German constitution mandates an equalizing redistribution across states, the distribution of education spending per pupil is relatively even across schools.

The enrollment share of private schools is quite small: between 5 and 6 percent in general education programs and 6 to 7 percent in vocational schools (Statistisches Bundesamt, 2000). Moreover, many private schools are heavily subsidized, so that private contributions usually cover only a small fraction of costs. About 7 percent of public expenditure on primary and secondary education is spent on private institutions (OECD, 1998). The relatively high share of primary and secondary school expenditures financed by private sources—some 24 percent—is somewhat misleading. It reflects mainly the German dual apprenticeship system, where general education in vocational schools is combined with training within firms (OECD, 1998). The private contributions mainly consist of firms' spending for training, which outweigh public expenditure on vocational schools.[15]

United States

Almost all children in the United States receive at least twelve years of schooling: six to eight years in elementary school, followed by four to six years in secondary school, typically graduating at the age of seventeen or eighteen. Middle schools serve children in intermediate grades between elementary and secondary schools. High school graduates may then choose to continue their education in technical or vocational institutions, two-year colleges, or four-year colleges or universities.

Administrative responsibility for public education at the elementary and secondary levels resides formally with the states. In many cases, much of the administrative and financial responsibility is delegated to local school districts. There are currently around 15,000 such districts, with large differences in size. In general, state boards coordinate large-scale activities, provide funding, administer achievement tests, and occasionally take over the administration of failing school districts, while local school districts make local funding decisions and run the schools.

In academic year 1999–2000, nearly half of public school revenues were funded by the states, just over 40 percent came from local sources, federal sources accounted for around 7 percent, and the remaining 3 percent came from private sources (National Center for Education Statistics, 2002, table 157). There is significant variation among the states in the division between state and local funding. In New Mexico and Vermont, local funding accounted for less than 20 percent of revenues in public schooling, while in Nevada and Illinois it accounted for about 60 percent. Average annual expenditure per student in public education exceeded $7,000 in 1999–2000, among the highest in the world. In this regard, too, there is considerable variation across states, with New York and New Jersey spending nearly $11,000 per pupil and Utah and New Mexico spending less than $5,000.[16]

The role of the state in funding education has increased over the past several decades, mainly as a result of judicial rulings that viewed large disparities in education spending, contingent on the wealth of the school district in which a child happens to reside, as being in violation of "equal protection" clauses in state constitutions. This principle was established by state supreme courts in two landmark cases—*Serrano v. Priest* in California in 1971 and *Robinson v. Cahill* in New Jersey in 1972—resulting in radical changes in the financing of public schools in these and many other states. Consequently, the states' share in education spending has increased over the last twenty-five years to the point that it now exceeds the share of local school revenues.

The share of private schools in enrollment has remained relatively stable in recent years, accounting for roughly 10 percent of the student body in elementary and high schools. Again, enrollment shares vary across states, from highs of just under 20 percent in Delaware and the District of Columbia to lows of under 3 percent in Utah and Wyoming. Over 80 percent of private school students attend denominational schools, of which Catholic schools account for the largest fraction.

Chile

Chile was the first Latin American country to introduce public education, in 1842 (Parry, 1997b). Compulsory education in Chile begins at age six and continues over a period of eight years of basic education, comprising six years of primary schooling and two years of lower secondary education, which is typically followed by four years of either general secondary education or a vocational program. On successful completion of either type of program, students obtain a certificate that allows them to enter higher education (OECD, 2000). In 1970, Chile achieved almost complete coverage in primary education, with literacy rates rising to 90 percent. Subsequently, secondary education enrollment rates also increased, from a level of 50 percent in 1970 to 82 percent in 1996 (Cox and Lemaitre, 1999).

Before 1980, financing and organization of public schools in Chile was centralized, and less than 25 percent of pupils enrolled in primary and secondary education attended private schools. In 1980, education reforms aimed at decentralizing the public system and encouraging privatization were initiated with the purpose of enhancing education quality through competition among schools (Gauri, 1998). The reforms effectively implemented a voucher system, allocating a fixed amount per student to any school, private or public, in which the student chose to enroll. In addition, responsibilities for curriculum development and organization of instruction were delegated to the school level, with the central government setting minimum standards (Parry, 1997a; OECD, 2000). As a result, more than 40 percent of all students enrolled in primary or secondary education attended a private school in 1996. Of these, about three fourths attended state-subsidized private schools. Only 9 percent of all pupils enrolled in 1996 attended private fee-paying schools that did not accept any government subsidies (Cox and Lemaitre, 1999). While the policy of equal subsidies per pupil was intended to allow students to attend private schools without paying tuition, entrance fees and monthly payments are still frequently observed. The government subsidy is reduced only if private funding exceeds half the value of the subsidy (Cox and Lemaitre, 1999). The central government provided over 90 percent of public education spending in 1990. Municipal funding, though providing only a further 5 percent, was sufficiently large to create visible differences in school budgets across municipalities (Parry, 1997b). About a third of public expenditures on primary and secondary education is spent on private institutions (OECD, 1998).[17]

New Zealand

Education in New Zealand is compulsory between the ages of six and sixteen and free until age nineteen. Compulsory education is mostly state-funded and state-owned but operates in a highly decentralized, market-based framework (Fiske and Ladd, 2000). Reforms initiated in 1989 under a plan known as "Tomorrow's Schools" transferred responsibility for operating the country's 2,700 elementary and high schools from the national Ministry of Education to boards of trustees that governed each school as an individual legal entity. Each board includes the school principal, parents, teachers, and community representatives and has considerable authority over school management. Further reforms enacted in 1991 did away with neighborhood enrollment zones, giving parents the right to choose which school their child would attend and forcing schools to compete for students in an educational marketplace. Funding is allocated by the number of students in the school, with targeted funding, introduced in 1995, tying about 20 percent of the budget to socioeconomic indicators such as household income, parents' occupation, crowding, remoteness, Maori and Pacific peoples' ethnicity, and so on.

The role of government is restricted to setting standards, purchasing education services, and monitoring outcomes. The Ministry of Education is entrusted with developing curriculum statements, allocating resources to schools, and monitoring effectiveness. A separate government department, the Education Review Office, monitors the general performance of the education system and reports to the public. A third, independent authority administers qualifications and oversees the examination system.[18] This leaves schools some leeway in determining their individual goals—for example, allowing minority schools to adopt curricula in which Maori culture, language, and values predominate[19]—and in designing programs to meet their declared objectives.

There are three types of schools in New Zealand. The large proportion, accounting for 87 percent of students in 1998, are state schools—owned by the state, receiving full state funding, extensively regulated, and prohibited from charging school fees to supplement government financing. A second type, accounting for 10 percent of enrollment, are schools that are privately owned but have been integrated into the state school system; they receive the same subsidies as state schools, accept a similar level of regulation, but may charge limited fees to cover the cost of capital investment. Private independent schools, accounting for the remaining 3 percent, receive lower subsidies, are less regulated, and may charge tuition, which indeed constitutes the major source of their income (LaRocque, 1999).

The new system of education that emerged from the Tomorrow's Schools initiative has been functioning for over a decade. It has achieved extensive decentralization, though perhaps not as extensive as its proponents envisioned, and some of the reforms have been scaled back. Open registration has recently been restricted, the large majority of schools follow narrowly prescribed curricula, and some schools in disadvantaged communities have failed to mobilize local communities and consequently have not served their students well. The system is still in a formative stage, striving to reconcile its guiding vision of local control, competition, and accountability with the fundamental ideal of an education system that promotes equal opportunity for all.

Conclusions

While early antecedents of public education can be found in ancient Greece and Judea, the modern development of public education begins with the Reformation, which attributed religious importance to education and viewed local churches and parishes as sharing parental responsibility for schooling. Locally administered public schools appeared sporadically as early as the sixteenth century, but education was not seen as a matter of wide public responsibility until the combined effect of the Enlightenment, the rise of the secular nation-state, and the Industrial Revolution led to the establishment and expansion of national education systems in western and central Europe and in North America, beginning in the late eighteenth century and through the nineteenth century, in which the state replaced the church as the dominant force in education. Free, compulsory schooling became widespread, financed from tax revenues, and large education administrations emerged to supervise school attendance, curricula, teacher training, certification and employment, capital investment and maintenance, and so on.

The twentieth century saw further reinforcement of these trends, as publicly operated and financed schools became the norm throughout the industrialized world and in many developing countries. This is evident in the dominant share of public funds in education spending, in the large fraction of students attending public schools, and in the active role of government administrations in regulating schools. Yet as public involvement in education becomes more extensive, counter-currents appear in many countries. They call for decentralization and greater autonomy of schools, more equitable distribution of school spending, greater choice for parents and more competition among schools, less hierarchical school systems that recognize the value of variety, a redefinition of the role of the state in religious education, greater accountability of schools for their performance, and so on— demands that are often in conflict with each other and raise intense debate.

3

Education, Growth,
and Distribution:
Empirical Evidence

Upon the education of the people of this country the fate of this country depends.
—Benjamin Disraeli, House of Commons (15 June 1874)

The seminal contributions of Schultz (1963) and Becker (1993/1964) established education as a key determinant of individual earnings, whether this is attributed to its role in building human capital, as they suggested, or to its function as a signaling or screening device, as Spence (1973) and others have maintained. On a macroeconomic level, numerous recent theoretical contributions since the influential work of Romer (1986) and Lucas (1988) have emphasized the role of human capital as an engine of growth. These both include *endogenous growth models*, following Romer and Lucas, which attribute long-run growth to increasing aggregate returns to education,[1] as well as *exogenous growth models* that extend the standard Solow (1957) model to include human capital (e.g., Mankiw et al., 1992). Both approaches interpret the commonly observed positive association between national income and education as evidence of its productive contribution.

Dissenting views interpret the evidence on education and income levels as indicating the opposite direction of causation—that higher incomes allow nations to achieve the higher levels of education to which they naturally aspire (Bils and Klenow, 2000). This view is supported by historical studies, which show how the democratizing effect of rising incomes led to the general expansion of public education, as part of the modern welfare state (Lindert, 1994; Justman and Gradstein, 1999). Of course, the two views are not mutually exclusive, and there is room to argue that increased levels of education are both the cause and effect of rising incomes.

The distribution of income also enters in this nexus of macroeconomic effects between growth and education. Early contributions following Kuznets's (1966) seminal work focused largely on the impact of income *levels* on the distribution of income, arguing that it is an empirical regularity that inequality follows an inverse U-shaped pattern—the *Kuznets curve*—in the course of development. Initially, inequality increases as income levels rise, peaking at some intermediate level of income and then falling with further increases in income levels.[2] This would seem to imply a tradeoff between inequality and growth at the early stages of development, but the contrast between the rapid industrialization of egalitarian economies in East Asia and the much weaker performance of Latin American economies with a much higher degree of inequality strongly indicates that this tradeoff can be avoided (Chenery et al., 1974).

This has led to empirical and theoretical work aimed at identifying the channels through which growth affects and is affected by the distribution of income. Addressing the role of education in this context, Galor and Zeira (1993) present a model in which the productivity of education depends on achieving some critical mass, which implies that at low levels of income some measure of inequality is necessary to achieve growth but at higher levels greater equality is beneficial, as it allows a larger number of households to reach the threshold level of education.[3] Political economy approaches stress the impact of income distribution on the allocation of public funds for education, on the one hand, and on the taxation of private income, on the other hand (Meltzer and Richard, 1981). These various approaches argue that not only the level of average income but also its distribution affect the aggregate level and distribution of current education investment, which shapes, in turn, the level and distribution of income in the future.[4]

This chapter presents empirical evidence on the relationship between education on the one hand and growth and income distribution on the other hand. We begin with evidence from Mincerian wage equations on private rates of return to investment in human capital and with an overview of the heated empirical debate on the link between education resources and achievements. We then go on to consider evidence on social returns to education derived from pooled cross-sectional wage equations and from macroeconomic data on the relation between income levels, growth, and education. Finally, we summarize empirical evidence on the relation between education and the distribution of income and between education and intergenerational mobility.

Investing in Education

The economic value of investments in education has been the subject of countless empirical studies. These studies have sought to estimate the economic returns from schooling to the individual and to society. Other research has studied the quantitative link between the amount of resources invested in education and scholastic achievement. Here we summarize the main conclusions that emerge from this research.

Private Returns

Modern studies of the private rate of return to education, drawing on the seminal contributions of Becker (1993/1964) and Mincer (1974), estimate the returns to education from the following "Mincerian" equation:

$$\ln w_i = \beta_0 + \beta_1 s_i + \beta_2 x_i + \beta_3 x_i^2 + \varepsilon_i, \tag{3.1}$$

where $\ln w_i$ is the natural log of the wage for individual i, s_i is years of schooling, x_i is experience, and ε_i is the disturbance term. The coefficient β_1 can then be conveniently interpreted as the rate of return to schooling, as it measures the proportional increase in earnings due to an extra year of schooling. A value of $\beta_1 = .10$ implies, for example, that an additional year of education is associated, ceteris paribus, with 10 percent higher earnings. These equations then allow one to construct age-earnings profiles for different education levels, from which an internal rate of return can be calculated after deducting costs.

There are, however, some difficulties in interpreting the estimated coefficient of education in the Mincer equation, which are susceptible to various biases. One source of bias that has received extensive attention is the omission of variables pertaining to individual ability from the regression specification. If abilities that have a positive impact on productivity in employment and that can be recognized by employers *independently of education* are positively correlated with education levels—possibly because they interact positively with education—then regression estimates are likely to overstate the rate of return to education.[5] Consequently, some recent studies have used "natural experiments" to better identify the return to education. One class of such experiments is provided by compulsory schooling laws, which introduce variability between people born earlier in the calendar year and entering school at an older age, and those born later in the year and entering school at a younger age (Acemoglu and Angrist, 2000). Another class of such experiments is obtained by studying wage differentials between differently educated identical twins, presumed to have the same innate "ability" (e.g., Ashenfelter and Rouse, 1998; Behrman and Rosenzweig, 1999).

In his extensive survey of the literature, Card (1995) reports a range of 4 to 10 percent in ordinary-least-squares (OLS) estimates of the private rate of return to education and 7 to 16 percent in estimates using instrumental variables. Ashenfelter, Harmon, and Oosterbeek's (1999) "metaanalysis" of 96 estimated rates of return compiled from 27 previous studies reached similar conclusions. They found an average return to schooling of 6.6 percent in 50 OLS estimates (with a standard deviation of 3.6), 9.3 percent in 35 instrumental variables estimates (standard deviation 4.1), and 9.2 percent in 11 estimates based on twins studies (standard deviation 3.7). Similarly, Acemoglu and Angrist (2000) report precisely estimated private returns to education of about 7 percent.

Several recent studies have found that the rate of return to education declines with the levels of education, so that education investment is more effective the younger the child. Carneiro, Heckman, and Manoli (2003) argue that investments made at preschool ages or at early stages of schooling have a significant effect in reducing potential criminal activity, forming social skills, and bringing the disadvantaged into the mainstream of the society. Referring to one such investment—the Perry Preschool program, which provided intensive help to disadvantaged preschoolers with subnormal IQ scores—Heckman (2000) found that with benefits measured through age twenty-seven, the program returned $5.70 for every dollar spent. In contrast, education investments in adolescents yield much smaller benefits and may not be cost-effective.

Social Returns
Social returns to education are much more difficult to measure than individual returns. The benefits of education are realized over a long period of time during which many other factors can affect economic performance. These effects can be reasonably controlled in large-sample studies of individual returns from education. There is much

less scope for controlling such effects at the country level. From a theoretical standpoint, social returns may exceed private returns due to positive externalities from education, as endogenous growth models assume, or fall below private returns if some measure of private returns derives from signaling.

A number of studies have estimated social returns realized in the market by augmenting the Mincerian equation with data on average levels of schooling in various locations. In contrast to the calculation of private returns, social returns should take into account the full resource cost of education on the cost side and gross rather than net earnings on the benefit side. Psacharopoulos (1981, 1994) estimated social rates of return to education at the national level based on international data, arriving at OLS estimates ranging between 5 and 15 percent and varying with the level of education and the country's stage of economic development. He found that returns to primary education are the highest among all educational levels, followed by secondary and then tertiary education, and are typically higher in developing countries than in more advanced countries. The size of the returns is roughly comparable to private returns.

Other econometric studies estimate the social rate of return to education at the municipal level using earning data in cities. Rauch (1993) reports statistically significant estimates of external effects from schooling in a cross-section of cities in the United States in 1980, finding that an increase of one year in average schooling in a city increases the average wages of individual workers in the city by around 4 percent. Moretti (2002) addresses the issue of endogeneity of average schooling using a sample of United States cities between 1980 and 1990. He also obtains significant values for the external effect, thus reinforcing Rauch's findings. Acemoglu and Angrist (2000) report a smaller, statistically insignificant external return of just over 1 percent, from an analysis of state-level variation in the United States.

These studies typically ignore nonmarket effects and hence cannot capture the full social returns to education. Haveman and Wolfe's (1984) survey of the literature indicated various channels through which education generates nonmarket effects: health and mortality benefits; reduced fertility; improved information and knowledge, which allow better consumption choices; greater productivity in the future production of human capital; a moderating effect on criminal activity; and a cohesive effect on the fabric of society. While these effects are extensively documented, they are difficult to quantify and attribute to specific investments in education, except in specific circumstances. One such study by Lochner and Moretti (2001) recently estimated that social savings deriving from the effect of high school graduation in reducing crime amount to between 14 to 26 percent of the private return to education. The shortage of quantitative evidence on the presence of significant spillover effects associated with human capital undermines the validity of theories of endogenous growth.

Resources and Schooling

While there is broad general agreement that education contributes to individual earnings and, as we show in the following section, to national prosperity, there remains substantial disagreement regarding the contribution of marginal increments in education spending to the quality of education. This controversy focuses on the relative importance of aggregate spending on education on the accumulation of human capital—compared to structural factors such as the ability to monitor teacher performance, the use of performance-based incentives, the competitive pressure of open enrollment, and so on. Theoretical analyses of education finance invariably assume that more educational resources generate higher levels of human capital, as does the analysis presented in this volume. It is therefore important to clarify the points of agreement and contention in this regard.

There seems to be no doubt that spending on education matters in an absolute sense. Thus, in international macroeconomic comparisons, especially those that include less advanced countries, more spending is typically associated with better educational outcomes. For example, a recent study compared literacy test scores among fifteen-year-olds in a selection of countries that included the OECD countries as well as several non-OECD middle-income countries. It found a positive association between test scores and the amount of spending per student, which explains more than 50 percent of the variation in test scores (OECD, 2003, PISA database, table 3.3). Furthermore, the Mincerian equations reviewed above suggest that applying resources to increase the years of education also yields high returns. The controversy is only whether a marginal increase in spending per student from its current levels in industrialized countries, especially in their more affluent communities, is likely to achieve a substantial gain in education quality and in future labor-market outcomes.

Considerable empirical effort has been directed toward estimating the effect of marginal increases in education resources, such as reduction in class size, on measures of education quality and labor-market prospects. Influential reviews of the empirical literature by Hanushek (1986, 2003) argue that the link between resources and outcomes is weak, pointing out, for example, that while real spending per student in the United States has increased for some time at an annual rate of over 3 percent, test scores have not shown any improvement since the 1960s. But Card and Krueger (1992, 1996) reach a more optimistic conclusion. Krueger's (1999) analysis of a controlled experiment that tested the effect of class size on student achievement in early elementary schooling in Tennessee ("Project STAR") found that class size had a significant effect on subsequent student achievement. Angrist and Lavy (1999), using exogenous variation in class size in Israel to identify class-size effects, also found a significant positive effect. However, evidence from international tests analyzed by Gundlach et al. (2001) and Woessmann (2003) indicated only weak, sporadic effects. Betts (1996), considering also the effect of education spending per student on labor-market outcomes, reaches a similar conclusion but finds that spending on additional years of schooling is cost-effective.

The Contribution of Human Capital to Growth

An alternative approach to estimating rates of return to education from individual earnings is to estimate the contribution of education levels to growth from macroeconomic regressions at the national level. The idea that human capital affects growth was first applied empirically by Denison in his attempt to understand the sources of modern economic growth. Much of the early literature was based on growth accounting analyses of time-series data, following Solow's (1957) seminal analysis, in which output growth is attributed to input growth and a residual. The contribution of education input is then gauged by measuring changes in the composition of the labor force by education levels weighted by income to assess the change in the quality-adjusted labor force, and multiplied by the share of the return to human capital in national income to obtain the proportion of output growth due to increased education. Assuming the national production function is

$$Y(t) = A(t)[K(t)]^{\alpha}[H(t)]^{\beta}[L(t)]^{1-(\alpha+\beta)}, \tag{3.2}$$

where Y is output, K is physical capital, H is human capital, and L is the size of the labor force, the contribution of enhanced human capital to the growth rate of output dY/Y is $\beta\, dH/H$.

This approach suffers from some of the weaknesses inherent in the rates-of-return literature. For one, it shares the implicit assumption that schooling differentials rather than unspecified differences in abilities are the source of variation in wages. Second, market wages are assumed to correctly reflect marginal products, thus ignoring possible externalities or signaling effects. This suggests that estimates based on this approach are likely to overstate the importance of education for growth. Griliches (1997), reviewing the growth accounting evidence, reached the conclusion that education is responsible for a third of the productivity residual in the United States in the postwar era; Maddison's (1991) study of four European countries, Japan, and the United States arrived at more modest estimates. It should be borne in mind that because education increases the stock of human capital only gradually, the full effect on output of an expansion of education services is felt only in the long run; recent growth is affected by the quality of education over the last generation. Using growth accounting methods to gauge the contribution of education to growth is appropriate only over long periods of time.

The recent availability of large sets of comparable international country-level data on output and investment—made possible by the development of notional exchange rates reflecting purchasing-power parity (Heston and Summers, 1991) and augmented by the systematic collection of comparative data on education (Barro and Lee, 1993)— has provided a new empirical basis for estimating the relationship between human capital and economic growth from extensive cross-country evidence. By using direct measures of national output and education attainment across countries to estimate the productivity of educational investment, the cross-country approach overcomes some of the limitations of the growth accounting and rate-of-return approaches, especially their assumption that wage differences reflect the marginal productivity of schooling.

There are essentially two approaches to estimating cross-country growth equations, differing in the source of growth. *Exogenous growth models* in the spirit of Solow's (1957) model assume constant returns to scale and consequently view growth as either an out-of-equilibrium phenomenon or as the result of exogenous residual factors often referred to generically as "technological progress." *Endogenous growth models*, following Romer (1986) and Lucas (1988), assume increasing returns to scale, which imply a positive rate of growth in the steady state.

An influential paper by Mankiw et al. (1992) estimates a variant of the Solow model augmented to include human capital and tests its implications with a view to showing that it can accommodate human capital as an explanatory variable, produce acceptable estimates of the partial elasticities, and approximate the dynamic process with reasonable accuracy; hence there is no need to introduce endogenous growth. The production function it specifies is of the form

$$Y(t) = [K(t)]^\alpha [H(t)]^\beta [A(t)L(t)]^{1-\alpha-\beta}, \tag{3.3}$$

where Y is output, H is the stock of human capital, K capital, L labor, and A the level of technology. It takes as given the fraction of the economy's output invested in physical capital, denoted q_k, and the fraction of income invested in human capital (including both direct costs and forgone earnings), denoted q_h. The evolution of the economy is then determined by

$$dk/dt = q_k y(t) - (n + g + \delta)k(t), \tag{3.4a}$$

$$dh/dt = q_h y(t) - (n + g + \delta)h(t), \tag{3.4b}$$

where $y(t) = Y/AL$ is output per effective unit of labor; $k(t) = K/AL$ is the stock of physical capital per effective unit of labor; $h(t) = H/AL$ is the stock of human capital per effective unit of labor; n is the average rate of growth of the working-age population; g is the rate of exogenous technological progress (that is, the growth rate of A); and δ is the rate of depreciation. Equations (3.4a) and (3.4b) implicitly assume a one-sector economy in which resources can be costlessly reallocated between consumption, investment in physical capital, and investment in human capital; and they assume that human capital depreciates at the same rate as physical capital.

If there are decreasing returns to the sum of human and physical capital (that is, if $\alpha + \beta < 1$), equations (3.4a) and (3.4b) imply that the economy converges to a steady state in which the levels of physical and human capital are given by

$$k^* = \left(\frac{q_k^{1-\beta} q_h^\beta}{n+g+\delta} \right)^{1/(1-\alpha-\beta)} \qquad h^* = \left(\frac{q_k^\alpha q_h^{1-\alpha}}{n+g+\delta} \right)^{1/(1-\alpha-\beta)}. \tag{3.5}$$

Substituting (3.5) into the production function and taking logarithms gives an equation for steady-state income per capita that depends on population growth and on the fraction of income invested in the accumulation of physical and human capital,

$$\ln\left[\frac{Y(t)}{L(t)}\right]^* = \ln A(0) + gt - \frac{\alpha + \beta}{1 - \alpha - \beta} \ln(n + g + \delta)$$

$$+ \frac{\alpha}{1 - \alpha - \beta} \ln(q_k) + \frac{\beta}{1 - \alpha - \beta} \ln(q_h), \tag{3.6}$$

or, alternatively, an equation in which income per capita is a function of the rate of population growth, investment in physical capital, and the *level* of human capital:

$$\ln\left[\frac{Y(t)}{L(t)}\right]^* = \ln A(0) + gt + \frac{\alpha}{1 - \alpha} \ln(q_k)$$

$$- \frac{\alpha}{1 - \alpha} \ln(n + g + \delta) + \frac{\beta}{1 - \alpha} \ln(h^*). \tag{3.7}$$

Note that in both equations it is the level of income that is being explained, not its growth rate.

Mankiw et al. (1992) estimate cross-country regressions for three subsamples of countries, regressing the log of income per capita on the log of the share of investment in GDP, the log of the rate of population growth plus 0.05 (taking 0.05 as the value of $g + \delta$), and the log of the percentage of the working-age population in secondary school, which is assumed to be proportional to q_h.[6] The regressions explain more than three quarters of the variance in two of the three subsamples considered,[7] show the schooling variable to be statistically significant, and indicate values of α and β in the vicinity of 1/3.

The dynamics of the model are approximated by noting that in the vicinity of the steady state the speed of convergence is given by

$$d \ln(y(t))/dt = \lambda[\ln(y^*) - \ln(y(t))], \tag{3.8}$$

where $\lambda = (n + g + \delta)(1 - \alpha - \beta)$ and y^* is the steady-state value of y derived from (3.6). This implies

$$\ln[y(t)/y(0)] = (1 - e^{-\lambda t})\frac{\alpha}{1 - \alpha - \beta} \ln(q_k) + (1 - e^{-\lambda t})\frac{\beta}{1 - \alpha - \beta} \ln(q_h)$$

$$- (1 - e^{-\lambda t})\frac{\alpha + \beta}{1 - \alpha - \beta} \ln(n + g + \delta)$$

$$- (1 - e^{-\lambda t}) \ln(y(0)), \tag{3.9}$$

which then serves as the basis for a regression equation in which the growth rate is the left-hand variable, and initial per capita output is added to the right-hand variables used in the previous estimation. This yields estimates between 0.56 and 0.80 for $\beta/(1 - \alpha - \beta)$, the elasticity of steady state per capita output with respect to the share of investment in human capital, from equation (3.6)—slightly lower than the estimated unitary elasticity of 1.00 implied by the estimated values $\alpha = \beta = 1/3$ obtained above. Assuming that education (including forgone income) accounts for 10 percent of GDP, and full adjustment to a new level of steady-state output is spread evenly over forty years— about the time it takes for full replacement of the workforce—these results imply an internal rate of return of 13.6 percent for OECD countries (from the growth-rate equation) and of between 20 percent (from the growth-rate equation) and 25 percent (from the growth-level equation) for a sample of ninety-eight countries that excludes large oil producers.[8] The estimate for the OECD countries is comparable in size to estimates obtained in the other methods described above; estimates for the larger sample are considerably higher.

Barro's (1991) panel analysis of real per capita GDP growth rates in roughly one hundred countries over three periods—1965 to 1975, 1975 to 1985, and 1985 to 1990—found that years of schooling in secondary and tertiary education for males age twenty-five and over have significant positive effects on growth. For instance, in the 1965 to 1975 sample, an increase in male secondary schooling of one standard deviation is estimated to raise the growth rate by 1.1 percentage points annually, with a similar increase in male higher education raising the growth rate by 0.5 percentage points.[9] Barro (2001) updates this analysis, adding more recent data and improved measures of educational attainment. The new results generally corroborate his earlier findings.

While findings of a significant positive relationship between the initial *level* of human capital and subsequent growth seem to be robust, several authors have noted a failure to detect a significant positive effect of annual *increments* in human capital on growth (e.g., Benhabib and Spiegel, 1994; Barro and Sala-i-Martin, 1995; Pritchett, 2001). The lack of such a relationship would appear to contradict the predictions of some endogenous growth models, such as Lucas (1988), which imply an explicit causal relationship between the rate of accumulation of human capital and growth and make it difficult to reconcile Mincerian microeconomic estimates of the productivity of investments in education with macroeconomic evidence. However, subsequent studies by Topel (1999) and Krueger and Lindahl (2001) argue that this failure should be attributed to improperly formulated econometric specifications. In particular, the latter study finds that when complementarity between human capital and physical capital is properly taken into account, changes in education attainment have a highly significant effect on growth, consistent with microeconometric Mincerian wage equations. Their study and the work of de la Fuente and Domenech (2000) on OECD data call attention to the measurement errors associated with proxies for human capital. In their analysis of an improved data set, de la Fuente and Domenech (2000) find a robust positive relationship between changes in levels of human capital and changes in output for a sample of OECD countries; and Hanushek and Kimko (2000) using students' test scores across a sample of (advanced) countries, as a quality measure of human capital, similarly discern a robust relationship to economic growth.[10] Research on this topic remains the subject of academic debate.

Education and Income Distribution

In this section, we first examine evidence regarding the relationship between education and intragenerational income distribution and then discuss the evidence pertaining to its effect on intergenerational mobility.

Education and Income Inequality

In an early work on the link between education and income inequality in the U.S. regional context, Becker and Chiswick (1966) show that inequality is positively correlated with inequality in schooling and negatively correlated with the average level of schooling. Subsequent studies, such as the cross-country analyses of Adelman and Morris (1973) and Chenery and Syrquin (1975), confirmed these findings, by and large, although Ram's (1984, 1987) slightly different specification failed to detect a significant relationship between mean schooling and schooling inequality on the one hand and income inequality on the other hand. More recently, Teulings and van Rens (2003) argue that because skilled and unskilled are imperfect substitutes in production, an increase in average education levels compresses the distribution of marginal productivity, which should lead to a more equal distribution of labor income. The authors test this hypothesis on the effect of education on income distribution in OECD countries and find support for it in their panel data.

More work done in this area examines the reverse effect of inequality on education. Perotti's (1996) important contribution on this issue regresses male and female secondary school enrollment ratios on a measure of inequality and a set of additional variables, including initial GDP and dummies for regional variables. He finds a robust negative effect: countries with a more equal income distribution tend to make larger investments in human capital. However, the precise channel that gives rise to this effect is not entirely clear, and Perotti offers two alternative explanations: one maintains that the positive effect of inequality on average fertility reduces average investment in human capital because of the quantity-quality tradeoff;[11] the other sees inequality working through credit constraints, which imply that in less equal societies more families are denied the opportunity of realizing their desired level of investment in human capital. While Perotti's evidence cannot distinguish between these two explanations, the negative effect of inequality on human capital investment is clearly identified and is robust. Subsequent work by Flug et al. (1998), DeGregorio and Kim (2000), and DeGregorio and Lee (2002), among others, provides further supporting evidence of this negative effect, emphasizing the significance of credit constraints. These findings accord well with the evidence in Psacharopoulos (1981, 1994) that returns to schooling are highest at the primary level and decrease with the level of schooling: fertility is higher and credit constraints are more acutely felt among low-income, poorly educated families.

Sylwester (2000) focuses more specifically on investment in public education, finding that higher levels of initial income inequality are associated with higher public expenditure on education. This reinforces previous findings of Easterly and Rebelo (1993) and James (1993), who similarly report that income inequality raises public expenditure on education. He also finds that democracies spend more than nondemocracies on education, as a percentage of GDP, suggesting that it is the political economy of education finance that drives support for public education in unequal societies.

Intergenerational Mobility

The human-capital model developed by Becker and coauthors, and especially its dynamic extension by Becker and Tomes (1979) and Loury (1981), forms the theoretical basis for economists' empirical estimation of intergenerational mobility, which has grown extensively over the past two decades.[12] Early estimates of intergenerational mobility tended to be quite low, but recent improved methodologies yield larger values. Becker and Tomes's (1986) empirical analysis presents evidence on the earnings or incomes of sons and fathers, bringing together three studies on the United States and studies on England, Sweden, Switzerland, and Norway. Their point estimates indicate that the elasticity of the son's income with respect to his father's income is under .20—that is, a 10 percent increase in the father's earnings (or income) raises the son's earnings by less than 2 percent. Behrman and Taubman (1985) find a similarly small intergenerational correlation. More recent studies by Solon (1992) and Zimmerman (1992), based on more representative samples and an improved methodology, find elasticities that are more than twice as large, over 0.40. These differences in estimates have important consequences for actual mobility rates. Consider two fathers, one of whom earns twice as much as the other. Ignoring possible differences in stochastic variation, if the intergenerational elasticity is 0.40, then the son of the richer father has an expected income that is 32 percent higher than the son of the poorer father, but if the elasticity is 0.20, then his expected income is only 15 percent higher; the corresponding values for the next generation are 12 and 3 percent.[13]

Focusing more specifically on mobility in education achievement, Kremer (1997) finds a correlation of 0.39 between the education achievements of parent and child in the United States. Checchi (1997) presents a comparative analysis of intergenerational income mobility in Germany, Italy, and the United States that indicates that the correlation between educational achievement and family background is weakest in the United States and strongest in Italy. Checchi, Ichino, and Rustichini (1999) reaffirm this conclusion as it applies to Italy and the United States and explain it through inherent differences in the school systems of the two countries—the greater centralization of the Italian school system versus the greater share of local finance in the United States and its larger share of private enrollment. The authors provide evidence that Italy, compared to the United States, displays less income inequality, as expected given the type of schooling system, but also less intergenerational mobility between occupations and between education levels.

These latter findings have been recently confirmed in the PISA 2000 study of scholastic achievement in the OECD countries (OECD, 2001b).

Overall, it detects a mildly positive relationship between family wealth and academic performance in a variety of subjects. This relationship is particularly strong in the United States (as well as in Brazil, Mexico, and Portugal) and comparatively weak in the Nordic countries, as well as in Austria, Belgium, Italy, Japan, Latvia, and Poland. The study also detects a similarly positive relationship between the education level of the parents (specifically, the mother) and the academic performance of the children.

Conclusions

In this chapter we presented a brief summary of some of the empirical evidence on the relationship between education and growth and income distribution, which will be relevant to the largely theoretical analyses of the following chapters. We began with the extensive evidence from Mincerian wage equations on private rates of return to investment in human capital, which indicated average rates of return in the vicinity of 6 to 7 percent based on OLS estimates and higher rates of 9 to 10 percent based on instrumental variable methods. We then considered evidence on social returns from pooled cross-sectional wage equations. International comparisons indicate OLS estimates between 5 and 15 percent and emphasize large variation in rates of return: returns are higher to primary education and in developing countries. Cross-sectional studies within the United States that use variation between cities or states to separate social and private returns yield ambiguous results, some indicating externalities of as much as 4 percent per year of schooling, with others finding only much smaller insignificant effects. Evidence on the quantitative relation between the amount of resources invested in education and scholastic achievement and labor market outcomes was also discussed. Whereas large differences in aggregate levels of physical and financial inputs obviously matter, as do years of schooling, there is considerable disagreement about whether marginal increases in class size or teacher salaries carry significant benefits.

A different approach to gauging the impact of education on growth and the distribution of income relates macroeconomic data on income levels and growth rates to measures of education levels and rates of accumulation. These studies also indicate a positive effect of education on growth, though estimates vary considerably with the method used. The reading of macroeconomic evidence on links between education,

income inequality, and intergenerational income mobility is more
tentative at the current stage of research. Cross-country studies of the
effect of inequality on schooling indicate that it has a negative effect on
overall education spending, though the channels through which this
effect works are yet to be identified. Similar evidence points to inequality exerting a positive effect on the share of public enrollment,
more so in democracies, presumably working through political channels. The few economic studies of the link between education and
intergenerational mobility indicate that centralized education systems
promote less mobile but more equal societies than decentralized systems. They affirm the importance of socioeconomic background for
academic achievement.

4 Political Determination of Education Spending

Nevertheless, in the most advanced countries the following will be generally applicable: . . .
10. Free education for all children in public schools.

—Karl Marx and Friedrich Engels, *Manifesto of the Communist Party* (1848)

In the preceding chapters we reviewed empirical evidence on the dominant role of the public sector in the supply of education and on the role of education as a determinant of aggregate growth and the distribution of income. This leads us now to turn to a series of formal models that explicitly incorporate political dimensions of public education in models of growth and distribution, in which the different preferences of heterogeneous individuals regarding public spending on education are aggregated through political mechanisms. Through these models we examine the implications of the political process for growth, income distribution, and mobility; compare different education regimes with regard to their popular support; and characterize the effect of the level and distribution of income on public investment in education.

This chapter introduces a two-period model that compares pure private and pure public education, predicated on two central assumptions: that households differ in their incomes (and, later, in other dimensions as well) and that credit constraints prevent parents from borrowing against the future earnings of their children. In subsequent chapters we incorporate elements of this model in explicitly dynamic models that allow us to characterize steady-state outcomes in the long run and in models of mixed regimes of private and public education.

A Basic Model of Private Education

We begin the formal presentation with a two-period model of *private education* as investment in human capital that will serve as a benchmark for subsequent analyses of public education.

Consider an economy populated with a unit measure of households indexed by i, each consisting of a parent and a child, in which all decisions are made by parents who determine the amount of investment in their children's schooling. Parent i's initial income y_i is exogenously given. We denote by F the cumulative distribution function (cdf) of income, and we assume that its mean Y exceeds its median y_m.[1]

Parents invest in their children's schooling from a "bequest motive," deriving utility from consumption c_i and from their offspring's net income y_{i1} in the next period.[2] Assigning the same utility function to all parents, we write $U(c_i, y_{i1})$ for parents' utility and assume it is twice differentiable, monotonically increasing, and quasi-concave. We also assume that the Inada conditions hold and that both goods are normal goods. To simplify the analysis at this point, we assume a linear production function[3] and choose units of measure so that the child's future income equals her human capital, $y_{i1} = h_i$, and equate the child's human capital with school spending per student, $h_i = s_i$, allowing us to write utility interchangeably as $U(c_i, s_i)$. This formulation abstracts from important issues regarding the relationship between school spending and the quality of schooling[4] and from differences in children's innate abilities, which we introduce later in this chapter. Parents then allocate their income between consumption c_i and education s_i, reflecting our assumption that credit constraints do not allow them to borrow against their children's future income. Normalizing all prices to unity, we have the budget constraint

$$y_i = c_i + s_i. \tag{4.1}$$

Under private schooling, utility maximization subject to constraint (4.1) yields the first-order condition $-U_c + U_s = 0$, where subscripts of functions denote partial derivatives: $U_c = \partial U / \partial c$ and $U_s = \partial U / \partial s$. Rearranging terms, this implies that the marginal rate of substitution (MRS) between schooling and consumption must equal the ratio of their respective prices, which equals one by our choice of units:

$$U_s / U_c = 1. \tag{4.2}$$

This condition and the budget constraint together determine the optimal amount of private education spending by parent i. If the credit constraint is binding and education is a normal good (as we have assumed), this amount is an increasing function of household income.

The constant-elasticity-of-substitution (CES) utility function is often used to model education demand:

$$U(c_i, s_i) = \begin{cases} c_i^{1-1/\sigma}/(1 - 1/\sigma) + \delta s_i^{1-1/\sigma}/(1 - 1/\sigma) & \text{if } \sigma \neq 1, \\ \ln c_i + \delta \ln s_i & \text{if } \sigma = 1, \end{cases} \tag{4.3}$$

where $\delta, \sigma > 0$, and σ is the elasticity of substitution between consumption and schooling.[5] Application of the first-order condition yields parent i's level of private-school spending $s_i = y_i \delta/(\delta^{1-\sigma} + \delta)$, which is proportional to income and thus implies that the income elasticity of demand for education quality is equal to one.

A Stone-Geary utility function allows a nonunitary income elasticity. It is defined by

$$U(c_i, s_i) = \begin{cases} (c_i - \underline{c})^{1-1/\sigma}/(1 - 1/\sigma) + \delta s_i^{1-1/\sigma}/(1 - 1/\sigma) & \text{if } \sigma \neq 1, \\ \ln(c_i - \underline{c}) + \delta \ln s_i & \text{if } \sigma = 1, \end{cases} \tag{4.4}$$

where $\delta, \sigma > 0$, and $\underline{c}$ may be either positive or negative; with $\underline{c} = 0$, the Stone-Geary specification reduces to the CES function. Applying the first-order condition, we obtain parent i's desired level of private school spending, $s_i = (y_i - \underline{c})\delta/(\delta^{1-\sigma} + \delta)$. In this case, the income elasticity of demand for schooling is $y_i/(y_i - \underline{c})$, which is greater than one (spending on education increases proportionately more than income) if $\underline{c}$ is positive and less than one if $\underline{c}$ is negative. The elasticity of substitution between consumption and schooling is less than σ if $\underline{c}$ is positive and greater than σ if $\underline{c}$ is negative.

Public Schooling

Now suppose that education is provided publicly. We focus here on the case of pure public education, excluding all private acquisition of education, and assume that public schooling is financed by a proportional income tax determined by majority voting among parents, where τ denotes the tax rate and $0 \leq \tau \leq 1$.[6] Household i's private consumption of other goods equals its after-tax income:

$$c_i = (1 - \tau)y_i, \tag{4.5}$$

and the proceeds of the tax are used to provide all children with a uniform level of schooling, which—assuming a balanced budget—equals

$$s_i = \tau Y \tag{4.6}$$

for all households. Public education severs the link between individual household income and the level of schooling. This is the principal feature that distinguishes public education from privately financed education.

With the education tax rate—or equivalently the amount of public schooling—determined by majority voting among parents, we define a tax rate to be in *political equilibrium* if it cannot be defeated by a majority of votes in pairwise comparison with any alternative tax rate.[7] To determine the outcome of this voting, we first obtain the preferred tax rate for parent i. Maximizing $U((1 - \tau)y_i, \tau Y)$ over τ yields the first-order condition $-y_i U_c + Y U_s = 0$. Rearranging terms, we have

$$U_s/U_c = y_i/Y, \tag{4.7}$$

where the left-hand side of the equation is the marginal rate of substitution between schooling and consumption, and the right-hand side is the *tax price* of public education for household i. Concavity of utility as a function of the tax rate ensures that the second-order condition for a maximum holds. Moreover, it implies that individual preferences are "single peaked"—that is, they have only one local maximum, which ensures that a majority voting equilibrium exists: there exists a tax rate to which no other tax rate is preferred by a majority of voters. This equilibrium tax rate equals the median of all preferred tax rates.[8]

Two opposing effects shape the impact of a voter's income on her preferred tax rate. Increased income generates an *income effect* that increases demand for education (as education is a "normal" good, demand for which increases with income) and leads the voter to support a higher tax rate, but at the same time it also raises the voter's tax price, generating a *substitution effect* that dampens demand for education and leads her to prefer a lower tax rate. The net impact of these two opposing effects depends on the parameters of the utility function.

The CES utility function illustrates this point. Applying the first-order condition (4.7) and rearranging terms, we obtain

$$\tau(y_i) = \delta/[(y_i/Y)^{\sigma-1}\delta^{1-\sigma} + \delta] \tag{4.8a}$$

for the preferred tax rate of household i. Thus the preferred tax rate is a monotonic function of the ratio between parental income and average income: a decreasing function of this ratio if the elasticity of substitution is greater than one and the substitution effect dominates the income effect and an increasing function if the elasticity of substitution is less than one and the income effect dominates. When the elasticity of substitution equals one—the logarithmic case—the two effects balance out, and the preferred rate is the same for all households, $\delta/(1+\delta)$. In all three cases, however, the preferred tax rate is monotonic in voter income, implying that the median-income household is decisive: the tax rate it prefers commands a majority over all other tax rates in pairwise comparison. The equilibrium τ^* is thus obtained by setting $y_i = y_m$ in (4.8a), and the uniform level of schooling equals $\tau^* Y$.

The ratio of mean income to median income is often used as an empirical measure of income inequality in the population. In the case of CES utility, the chosen tax rate is a decreasing function of this measure of inequality if the elasticity of substitution is less than one and an increasing function if the elasticity of substitution is greater than one.[9] In both cases, the tax rate does not vary with proportional changes in the general level of income in the population that do not affect the ratio of mean to median income.

The Stone-Geary utility function allows the possibility of a non-monotonic relationship between income and the preferred tax rate. Again, application of the first-order condition (4.7) to the utility function in (4.4) determines the preferred choice of the education tax rate, which in this case equals

$$\tau(y_i) = [(y_i - \underline{c})/y_i]\delta/[(y_i/Y)^{\sigma-1}\delta^{1-\sigma} + \delta]. \tag{4.8b}$$

The second-order condition always holds, so that individual preferences over taxes are single-peaked. To see how the preferred tax is affected by individual income, note that its derivative with respect to y_i is positive if and only if $\sigma < 1/[1 - \underline{c}/y_i\tau(y_i)]$. Then if the income elasticity of school demand is no less than one and the elasticity of substitution is less than one ($\underline{c} \geq 0$ and $\sigma < 1$), the preferred tax rate is everywhere increasing in income; and if the income elasticity of school demand is no greater than one and the elasticity of substitution is greater than one ($\underline{c} \leq 0$ and $\sigma > 1$), then the preferred tax rate is everywhere decreasing in income. In both these cases, the median-income voter is decisive, and the chosen tax rate is the tax rate preferred by the median-income household, obtained by setting $y_i = y_m$ in (4.8b). However, if neither condition holds—for example, if $\sigma > 1$ and $\underline{c} > 0$— then the preferred tax rate is not monotonic in income, and the median-income voter may not be decisive. The relation between in-equality and the tax rate depends, as in the CES case, on the elasticity of substitution. But as distinct from the CES case, the tax rate is sensi-tive to proportional changes in the incomes of all households: it increases with a proportional increase in all incomes if c is positive and decreases with a proportional increase in incomes if c is negative.

Empirical Evidence on Income and Substitution Elasticities

The preceding discussion highlights the effect of income and substitu-tion elasticities on public spending on education. There is an extensive empirical literature aimed at measuring their magnitudes.

Early estimates of the income elasticity of education demand were summarized by Bergstrom et al. (1982) as indicating that the income elasticity of demand for public education "is on the order of 2/3," but more recent estimates suggest slightly higher values. At the higher end are Romer et al.'s (1992) estimates derived from a detailed study of spending and voting in New York school districts, which indicate an income elasticity of public spending per student slightly less than one. Fernandez and Rogerson's (2001) estimates based on a pooled cross-section of state-level data over four decades, which control for demo-graphic composition, find a value of about 0.90, and Poterba (1997) estimates a value of 0.75, also from state-level data. Cohen-Zada and Justman (2003), calibrating income and substitution elasticities from private enrollment rates, find a range of values between 0.71 and 0.88.

Attempts to estimate the price elasticity of demand for private education directly from microdata by regressing individual schooling decisions on private tuition levels are difficult to interpret because they implicitly assume that education quality is independent of tuition. Long and Toma (1988) and Buddin et al. (1998) failed to identify a sig-nificant price effect, while Lankford and Wyckoff (1992) found large, significant elasticities: -0.92 for elementary education and -3.67 for secondary education. Indirect measures have produced more consis-tent results. Fernandez and Rogerson (1999) calibrate the elasticity of substitution from variation in spending levels across school districts in California, finding a range of values between -0.80 and -0.95, and Cohen-Zada and Justman's (2003) calibration of the elasticity of substi-tution from private enrollment rates indicates a range of values be-tween -1.10 and -1.35.

These results, indicating that the income and substitution elasticities are similar in magnitude and therefore roughly balance out, accord with direct estimates of the tax-price elasticity of spending per student, which are generally small in magnitude. A series of careful studies by Bergstrom et al. (1982), Rubinfeld et al. (1987), and Rubinfeld and Shapiro (1989) used qualitative survey responses directly to determine the effect of individual income on the desired level of public spending. The net effects they found were small in magnitude and statistically insignificant while varying in sign.[10] This is consistent also with the earlier studies summarized by Bergstrom et al. (1982).

Taken together, these studies indicate that while the income elasticity may be slightly smaller in magnitude than the elasticity of substitution, implying a moderate negative effect of individual income on the desired level of the education tax rate, both elasticities are close to one. This suggests that a logarithmic utility function, which imposes both a unitary elasticity of substitution and a unitary income elasticity—and hence a zero tax-price elasticity—can provide a reasonable approximation for many applications, while greatly simplifying the analysis.

Differences in Abilities

The preceding theoretical analysis ignores differences in abilities across individuals, taking spending on education as the sole source of income heterogeneity. Now we modify this assumption, allowing variations among individuals in their ability to translate formal schooling into earnings. This will enable us to model intergenerational mobility—the effect of socioeconomic origins on education and earnings.

The empirical evidence, some of which we review in chapter 3, indicates significant statistical correlation between parental schooling and earnings on the one hand and the schooling and earnings of the child on the other hand. Formal schooling is only one component in the formation of human capital. A significant part of human-capital accumulation takes place outside schools through interactions with family members, friends, clubs, and so on. Psychological research has established that much of human cognitive ability is shaped at very early stages of development, implying that the preschool environment, most significantly in the family, plays an important role in forming human capital.[11] This role can partly be ascribed to the ability of more affluent parents to provide their children with "tradable" education inputs available on the open market: a congenial physical environment, books, a computer, private lessons, and so on. However, some of the advantages offered by a better home environment are "nontradable"— cultural and ethical values that cannot be purchased, as well as genetically transmitted characteristics that may bear on education achievement and earnings.[12] Studies on identical twins have sought to separate the effect of genetic factors from the home environment, but from a policy viewpoint the more relevant distinction is between "tradable" and "nontradable" inputs (Gilboa, 2003).

To introduce innate abilities as simply as possible, suppose that parental abilities a_{i0} are exogenously given and that the child's ability a_{i1} is determined by the combined effect of parental ability and a random disturbance, b_i:

$$a_{i1} = a_{i0}{}^{\gamma} b_i{}^{1-\gamma}, \tag{4.9}$$

where $0 < \gamma < 1$ measures the relative importance of the parental input in affecting child's ability, whether through nature or nurture. The smaller γ is, the less important socioeconomic background is, and the greater the degree of intergenerational mobility is: if γ is close to 0, parental input is immaterial, while if it is close to 1, there is almost perfect intergenerational correlation of abilities. As we shall see further on, the relative importance of parental input bears directly on the relative efficiency of public education. The child's human capital h_i is taken as the product of her innate ability a_{i1} and formal schooling s_i: $h_i = a_{i1} s_i$. Parental utility is then a function of consumption and the child's human capital $U(c_i, h_i)$, which we equate, as above, with earnings. The parent's budget constraint $y_i = c_i + s_i$ can then be written as $y_i = c_i + h_i/a_{i1}$, which shows $1/a_{i1}$ to be the relative price of acquiring human capital for a child with ability a_{i1}. Finally, we assume for simplicity that parents know the ability of their children at the time that schooling decisions are made and that there exists a nonnegative correlation between parents' initial incomes and their own abilities.

Under *private* schooling, with CES utility the share of income spent on schooling is $\delta/[(a_{i1}\delta)^{1-\sigma} + \delta]$, which does not depend on income but does vary with the ability of the child. If the elasticity of substitution is less than one, then more is spent on the education of less able children to partially compensate for their lower ability; if it is greater than one, then more is spent on abler children to take advantage of their higher ability. Only in the case of logarithmic utility, when the elasticity of substitution equals one, is the share of income spent on schooling constant and equal to $\delta/(1 + \delta)$.

Now consider *public* education financed by a proportional tax determined by majority vote. To obtain the preferred tax rate for parent i, recall that $c_i = (1 - \tau)y_i$, and $h_i = a_{i1}\tau Y$, so that from the first-order condition we have

$$U_h/U_c = y_i/(a_{i1}Y). \tag{4.10}$$

Concavity then ensures that the second-order condition for a maximum holds and implies that individual preferences are single peaked; hence a majority voting equilibrium exists and the median preferred tax rate is the equilibrium outcome. With a CES utility function, applying the first-order condition and rearranging terms yields

$$\tau(y_i) = \delta/[(y_i/a_{i1}\delta Y)^{\sigma-1} + \delta]. \tag{4.11}$$

The preferred tax rate is a monotonically decreasing function of the ratio between parental income and the child's ability y_i/a_{i1}, if the elasticity of substitution is less than one, and is a monotonically increasing function if the elasticity of substitution is greater than one. Again, in the logarithmic case, when the elasticity of substitution equals one, the preferred tax rate is uniformly $\delta/(1 + \delta)$.

To characterize the voting equilibrium, note that the preferred tax rate is a function of the ratio of the parent's income to the child's ability and hence is constant along rays in (the positive orthant of) the income-ability plane. These have the general form $a_{i1} = \lambda y_i$ for positive values of λ. Denoting the joint density function of parental ability and child's income by $f(y_i, a_{i1})$, the equilibrium tax rate is determined by finding the value of λ^* that solves

$$\int_0^{\lambda^*} \int_0^{\infty} f(y, \lambda y)\, dy\, d\lambda = 1/2 \tag{4.12}$$

and substituting λ^* for a_{i1}/y_{i0} in (4.11).

Comparing Public and Private Education in the Short Run

We can now compare the short-run effects of pure public and pure private education in the context of our theoretical framework. Of course, actual education systems only rarely approximate either of these two extremes, and comparing such systems in practice will depend more on their specific structure than on whether they are labeled "public" or "private." Locally financed public education, for example, may be less egalitarian than private schools financed by a national voucher system. We expand on mixed systems of education and on the link between local education and residential location in subsequent chapters. The purpose of the present comparison is to highlight the underlying forces at work.

One immediate result of our analysis is that public education both reduces the level of income inequality in the next generation and increases intergenerational mobility. Under private education, the education a child receives is constrained by the parents' resources, as parents cannot borrow against the future earnings of their children, and hence is more closely correlated with parental income. Public education weakens this link by providing a uniform level of schooling, which the rich subsidize to the advantage of the poor. However, even under public education income differences persist from one generation to the next and are correlated across generations because of the correlation between ability and parental income. An explicitly stochastic exposition of this point is provided in an appendix to this chapter.

Because different families are differently affected by the adoption of public schooling, some may support it while others reject it. The introduction of public education depends on gainers carrying greater political weight than losers.[13] Public support for the two regimes is most easily compared in the case of logarithmic utility. As the preceding analysis indicates, the share of resources devoted to education is the same under both regimes, but its incidence differs. Under private education, spending on education is proportional to individual household income, while under public education it is proportional to the average income in the economy. Thus, the poorer the household, the more it benefits from public education. Under logarithmic utility, consumption in each household is the same under both regimes, but households earning above-average income acquire a better education for their children under the private regime, while households earning below-average income receive a better education under a public regime. Thus households earning above-average income are better off under private education, while those earning below-average income do better under public education.[14] Hence, the extent of political support for public education hinges on the political power of low-income voters. In a democracy in which all households have the same political weight, the median-income household will be decisive, and as the median is generally below the mean, public education should command a majority. However, if the political process excludes the poorest individuals or offers them less than proportional influence, public education may not enjoy decisive support.[15]

The preceding analysis focuses on the distribution of income as a crucial factor affecting public choice between public and private schooling, but other factors may also play important roles. Theoretical analyses often point to production externalities as a primary reason for public involvement in education, although the empirical evidence on this point, briefly reviewed in chapter 3, is not clear-cut. Social returns on investment in human capital are more difficult to measure than private returns, and it is not clear that they exceed private returns at current schooling levels in developed countries.[16] To the extent that positive externalities exist, they increase support for public schooling, which allows external benefits to be internalized. At the same time, financing public education from taxes creates an excess burden, which diminishes its value.

Among other important factors that bear on the comparison between private and public schooling is the relative productive inefficiency of public education and the strength of religious sentiment.[17] Proponents of private operation of schools publicly funded through vouchers have repeatedly maintained that publicly operated schools are generally inefficient due to a lack of competition and entrepreneurship. There is an extensive empirical literature concerned with measuring the impact of private competition on the quality of public schooling. Religious belief is another factor in the comparison between public and private education. In the United States, religious schools account for over 80 percent of private enrollment. While there is some evidence that religious schools achieve better scholastic outcomes than public schools, there remain identification issues that have not been fully resolved. Moreover, religious sentiment introduces a subjective dimension in evaluating school quality that varies among households. Parents judge a private parochial school not only on the strength of the test scores it achieves but also on how they value the particular religious environment it offers.

Education and Redistribution

Our analysis of the income-equalizing consequences of public education identified reasons why the poor should support public education and the rich oppose it. Indirectly, however, the equalizing aspect of public education may benefit the rich as well, insofar as it reduces future demand for income redistribution, which may have a destabilizing effect. This section focuses on the role of public education in alleviating anticipated demands for redistribution that result from income—or, more generally, social—disparities. Its underlying assumption is that high levels of income inequality may have undesirable efficiency consequences. In an ordered democratic society, these mostly take the form of redistributive legislation that increases the excess burden of taxation; in other cases, redistribution may take a violent form. This effect was highlighted in the seminal work of Meltzer and Richard (1981) and later elaborated in Alesina and Rodrik (1994), Persson and Tabellini (1994), and others. In this context, uniform public education can benefit all voters by smoothing out income differences and thus moderating claims for subsequent redistribution of income.

To illustrate how voters' preferences between public and private schooling are affected by the presence of potential redistributional conflict, we add to the two-period model described above an additional stage in which next-generation income may be redistributed, following Gradstein (2000). Suppressing variation in abilities, assume that the future gross income of the child in household i is linear in her current schooling and equal to As_i, where $A > 0$ is a common constant; and let S denote the average level of schooling in her cohort. Furthermore, assume that whatever the education regime, net income in the second generation is subject to peaceful, democratic redistribution. Following Meltzer and Richard (1981), we posit a balanced-budget redistributive policy characterized by the proportional tax rate $\eta \geq 0$, which is offset by a lump-sum transfer, so that after-tax income in the second generation equals

$$y_{i1} = [(1 - \eta)As_i + \eta AS].$$ (4.13)

The larger the value of η, the greater the degree of redistribution from the rich to the poor in the second generation: when $\eta = 0$, there is no redistribution at all, and redistribution becomes more progressive as η increases. Suppose also that there is an upper bound on redistribution $\bar{\eta}$ that bounds it away from 100 percent, so that $0 \leq \eta \leq \bar{\eta} < 1$.[18]

The sequence of events—under either education regime—is then as follows. Initially, in the first generation, parents allocate their budgets between consumption and schooling, either individually under private education or collectively under public education. These schooling decisions then generate second-generation pretax income. Finally, a redistributive tax rate is chosen by majority voting in the second generation, which determines after-tax income. In equilibrium, parents are assumed to correctly anticipate future redistribution in determining their children's level of schooling.

Solving the model recursively, note that the next-generation voter's position with regard to the desired value of redistribution is such that individuals with income below the mean desire $\eta = \bar{\eta}$, while those above it desire $\eta = 0$. When education is purely public and schooling is uniform, next-generation pretax incomes are identical, and so there is no incentive for income redistribution, and gross and net incomes coincide. In contrast, when education is purely private, all individuals with education levels below the mean want maximal redistribution. Assuming that first-generation income is conventionally skewed so that the majority of households earn less than average income and the majority of children have less than average schooling, the equilibrium value of the redistribution parameter equals its maximal bound $\bar{\eta}$.

If this bound is large enough, all parents prefer public to private education. Assume that $\bar{\eta} = 1$.[19] Then under private education, $\eta = \bar{\eta}$ is chosen, and after-tax income, given by (4.13), is independent of individual human capital. But then investment in human capital carries no return and will not be undertaken under a private-schooling regime, resulting in low utility levels. More generally, the income inequality created by private schooling induces political pressure for more redistribution, and the anticipation of this greater redistribution leads parents to invest less in their children's schooling, thus decreasing the amount of human capital and output in the next generation. In contrast, public education, by equalizing incomes, reduces future redistribution thereby ensuring a higher return from schooling, from which all individuals benefit, rich as well as poor. Time-consistent human-capital accumulation under private schooling is inefficient in this case.

In a related vein, Gradstein and Justman (2000) consider the potential for redistributional conflict that arises as a result of cultural rather than income differences. In this model, education has an ethnic dimension. When individuals belong to different cultural groups, private education preserves cultural differences over time. These differences are assumed to result in intergroup redistributional tensions, whereby each group expends resources to capture a fraction of the other group's income. This leads to a waste of resources. To the extent that public education instills common values, it has the potential to reduce redistributional pressures among different cultural groups. This role of education is considered in greater detail in chapter 8.

A less peaceful channel for redistribution is examined by Grossman (1991, 1994), which highlights the adverse effect of an unequal distribution of wealth that creates incentives for the poor to engage in "appropriative" rather than productive activities. The adverse implications of appropriative activities for growth are described in Lane and Tornell (1996), Tornell (1997, 1999), and Benhabib and Rustichini (1996), among others. In more extreme cases, redistributional conflicts resulting from deep differences in income and wealth may take the form of sociopolitical instability, a tenet of Marxist analysis borne out by dramatic historical examples as well as systematic statistical evidence. Empirical evidence on the link between income inequality and redistributive tension is provided by Perotti (1996), Alesina and Perotti (1996), and Svensson (1998). In related work, Acemoglu and Robinson (2000, 2001) argue that an oligarchy may find it in its best interest to reduce or eliminate the threat of political instability by pursuing more egalitarian policies.[20]

A different link between education and redistribution is often referred to as the *Samaritan's dilemma* and derives from a redistribution model based on altruism. Suppose, as in Bruce and Waldman (1991), that the government has an altruistic regard for the poor, causing it to transfer income from rich to poor in each period. This creates a disincentive for poor parents to invest in the education of their children in the form of a moral hazard: returns from education are partially offset by the loss of transfer revenues. Consequently, the poor underinvest in human capital. In these circumstances, mandating a minimal level of education may cause a Pareto improvement. Relatedly, Boadway et al. (1996) posits that individuals differ with respect to their productive abilities, and these differences are positively correlated with their capacity to benefit from education, so that a given amount of human-capital investment yields a higher return for a more able individual than for a less able one. In a time-consistent equilibrium, a benevolent government imposes high redistributive taxes on returns to human capital, which provides disincentives for investment in education. Again, mandatory education may be beneficial in this case.

Conclusions

This chapter presented a basic toolbox for analyzing the political economy of education, which we use in subsequent chapters. They highlight egalitarian features of public schooling, which imposes a disproportionate share of its fiscal burden on the more affluent sectors of society while aiming to provide a uniform level of education to all. Hence, the adoption of public education hinges, to some extent, on the political influence of the poor, as they have more reason to support it. Yet the more affluent may also find indirect advantages in a public education system that alleviates social tensions and reduces political pressure for redistribution. In the next chapter, we elaborate on these issues and consider the different effect of public and private education on growth, distribution, and intergenerational mobility in the long run.

Appendix 4.1 Voting Equilibria

Consider an individual acting as an economic agent and making utility-maximizing voting decisions on a policy parameter τ, given a set of characteristics a^i (possibly a vector). The assumption that the policy parameter is unidimensional is an obvious limitation, which fails to hold in many actual cases but is widely used. Two-dimensional voting problems often do not have political equilibria.

Let $V(\tau, a^i)$ denote the agent's indirect utility as a function of the value of the policy parameter and her individual traits. The preferred parameter value of voter i is then defined by

$$\tau(a^i) = \text{Argmax}_\tau \, V(\tau, a^i). \tag{4.14}$$

A particular aggregation rule that transforms individual preferences into policy decisions is given by majority voting, which is defined as follows:

Definition 4.1 A majority voting equilibrium is a policy τ^* that is never rejected by a majority of voters in a pairwise comparison with any alternative policy.

The Condorcet paradox, discovered by the Marquis de Condorcet at the end of the eighteenth century, indicates that, in general, such equilibrium outcomes may fail to exist. Mueller (1989, ch. 5) presents a detailed discussion of this paradox, its generalizations and implications. This finding has spawned interest in characterizing the circumstances under which existence of voting equilibrium is ensured. One such condition, single-peakedness, was first iterated in a well-known paper by Black (1948).

Definition 4.2 Voter i's preferences are single-peaked if either $\tau'' \leq \tau' \leq \tau(a^i)$ or $\tau'' \geq \tau' \geq \tau(a^i)$ always implies $V(\tau'', a^i) \leq V(\tau', a^i)$.

Black's existence theorem then goes as follows:

Theorem 4.1 If all voters' preferences over a given ordering of policy alternatives are single-peaked, then a majority voting equilibrium exists and coincides with the median-ranked policy alternative.

This result, though derived under the somewhat simplistic assumptions of unidimensionality and single-peakedness, is nevertheless widely used in a variety of political economy models; Persson and Tabellini (2000, ch. 2) present a rich selection of such examples. Most of the models considered below satisfy these assumptions and hence enable a straightforward application of Black's theorem.

Where these assumptions are not satisfied, an alternative property, referred to as *single crossing of preferences*, can been evoked. This property, first discovered in Roberts (1977) and generalized more recently in Gans and Smart (1996), is closely related to the Spence-Mirrlees condition on marginal rates of substitution. It assumes that the individual characteristics a^i are also unidimensional.

Definition 4.3 Voter i's preferences satisfy the single-crossing property if $\tau(a^i)$ is a monotonic function.

The existence result then follows:

Theorem 4.2 If all voters' preferences satisfy the single-crossing property, a majority voting equilibrium exists and coincides with the preferred policy of the voter with the median value of a^i.

If households can choose between public and private education after the tax rate is determined (Epple and Romano, 1996a) or if an additional source of variation in the demand for education, besides income, is introduced (Epple and Sieg, 1999), existence of an equilibrium is not ensured. We expand on this in chapter 7.

Appendix 4.2 A Stochastic Model

Assume that parental income is distributed lognormally in the population, $\ln y_i \sim N(\mu_y, \sigma_y^2)$, and that the ability of the child satisfies

$$\ln a_i = \ln y_i + u_{ai}, \tag{4.15}$$

where u_a is an i.i.d. disturbance term, normally distributed with variance σ_{ua}^2 and zero mean. Assuming that parental utility is a logarithmic function of consumption and school spending and that parents cannot borrow against their children's future income, under private schooling parents spend a fixed proportion of their income on their children's education:

$$s_i = [\delta/(1+\delta)]y_i. \tag{4.16}$$

The child's human capital is then a function of her innate ability and of parental investment in education:

$$\ln h_{i,pr} = \ln a_i + \gamma \ln s_i = \gamma \ln[\delta/(1+\delta)] + (1+\gamma)\ln y_i + u_{ai} \tag{4.17}$$

after substitution. Then $\ln h_i$ is also normally distributed, with mean and variance

$$\mu_{h,pr} = \gamma \ln[\delta/(1+\delta)] + (1+\gamma)\mu_y, \tag{4.18}$$

$$\sigma_{h,pr}^2 = (1+\gamma)^2\sigma_y^2 + \sigma_{ua}^2, \tag{4.19}$$

and the correlation between parental income and the child's human capital under private education is

$$\rho_{yh,pr} = (1+\gamma)\sigma_y/\sigma_h. \tag{4.20}$$

Under public education, school spending is uniform for all households and equals

$$s_{pu} = [\delta/(1+\delta)]Y_0 = [\delta/(1+\delta)]\exp(\mu_y + \sigma_y^2/2), \tag{4.21}$$

creating human capital

$$\ln h_{i,pu} = \ln a_i + \gamma \ln s_{pu}$$

$$= \gamma \ln[\delta/(1+\delta)] + \ln y_i + \gamma(\mu_y + \sigma_y^2/2) + u_{ai} \tag{4.22}$$

with mean and variance

$$\mu_{h,pu} = \gamma \ln[\delta/(1+\delta)] + (1+\gamma)\mu_y + \gamma\sigma_y^2/2, \tag{4.23}$$

$$\sigma_{h,pu}^2 = \sigma_y^2 + \sigma_{ua}^2 < \sigma_{h,pr}^2, \tag{4.24}$$

and the correlation between parental income and filial human capital under public education is

$$\rho_{yh,pu} = \sigma_y/\sigma_h < \rho_{yh,pr}. \tag{4.25}$$

Thus compared to private education, public education results in less inequality and a smaller correlation between the income of parent and child, implying greater social mobility.

5   Dynamic Models of Education

They should observe what elements mingle in their offspring; for if the son of a golden or silver parent has an admixture of brass and iron, then nature orders a transposition of ranks, and the eye of the ruler must not be pitiful towards the child because he has to descend in the scale and become a husbandman or artisan, just as there may be sons of artisans who having an admixture of gold or silver in them are raised to honour, and become guardians or auxiliaries. For an oracle says that when a man of brass or iron guards the State, it will be destroyed.

—Plato, *The Republic*, Book 3, 415

In this chapter we consider the long-run implications of public financing of education by extending the two-period analyses of the preceding chapter to infinitely many periods. This sheds light on the long-run impact of public education on steady-state growth, income distribution, and intergenerational mobility and its wide currency as the "great equalizer" of economic opportunity.[1]

The point of departure for our analysis is a variation on the Solow-type neoclassical growth model, with human capital as the vehicle of growth. However, our approach differs from standard neoclassical growth models in two important respects, introduced in the preceding chapter. It is not a "representative agent" model but rather allows heterogeneity in family income and in the ability to translate schooling into earnings.[2] And it does not assume well-functioning financial markets that would allow the level of investment in education to be determined only by its marginal productivity: it posits that parents cannot borrow against the future earnings of their children, so that private education is exclusively financed from parental income. When capital markets are perfect, the initial distribution of income is immaterial for subsequent accumulation of human capital, whatever the education regime. In contrast, when human capital is self-financed, initial income differences constrain investment in human capital under private education, possibly reducing aggregate production efficiency and perpetuating income inequality.

A Dynamic Economy

We begin by extending the static framework described in the preceding chapter for the benchmark case of private schooling. As before, we assume that in each period t the economy is populated by a unit measure of households indexed by i, that each household consists of a parent and child, and that parents make all decisions in the economy. Parents derive utility from consumption and from their children's income, $U(c_{it}, y_{it+1})$. Positing a constant elasticity of substitution (CES) utility function, we write

$$U(c_{it}, y_{it+1}) = c_{it}^{1-1/\sigma}/(1 - 1/\sigma) + \delta y_{it+1}^{1-1/\sigma}/(1 - 1/\sigma), \tag{5.1}$$

where δ and σ are positive constants, and σ is the elasticity of substitution, with $\sigma = 1$ corresponding to a logarithmic specification. The income of parent i in period t is denoted by y_{it}, and the distribution of income in period t is described by the cumulative distribution function (cdf) F_t. The distribution of income in the initial period is exogenously determined. We assume initially that innate abilities are equal.

A Basic Model of Private Education

Under private education, household spending on education is entirely self-financed. In each period $t > 0$, the parent of household i allocates her income between consumption c_{it} and spending on private schooling s_{it+1}, satisfying the budget constraint

$$y_{it} = c_{it} + s_{it+1}. \tag{5.2}$$

Next-period income y_{it+1} is then produced via the linear production function:

$$y_{it+1} = As_{it+1}, \tag{5.3}$$

where $A > 0$ is a technology parameter, which we assume for simplicity to be constant across individuals and over time. Maximizing utility (5.1) subject to the budget constraint (5.2) and the production function (5.3), we obtain household i's optimal amount of private schooling, $s_{it+1} = \omega y_{it}$, where $\omega = \delta/[(A\delta)^{1-\sigma} + \delta]$ is the share of education spending in income, which yields utility

$$U_{it} = [y_{it}^{1-1/\sigma}/(1 - 1/\sigma)][(1 - \omega)^{1-1/\sigma} + \delta(A\omega)^{1-1/\sigma}]. \tag{5.4}$$

The growth rate of dynasty i's income is $y_{it+1}/y_{it} = A\omega$, so that all dynasties' incomes grow at the same rate, implying that this must also be the growth rate of the economy as a whole. Moreover, as income shares do not change over time, income inequality remains constant (in the sense that the Lorentz curve is constant). And as the child's income is perfectly correlated with the parent's income, we can say that there is no (relative) intergenerational income mobility in this case.

Poverty Traps

These conclusions change markedly when some of the assumptions are modified. The shape of the production function that translates resources invested in education into output is an important example in this regard. In the preceding analysis we assumed that the marginal product of education does not increase when the level of education increases. If instead there is an initial increase—for example, if there is some threshold level of schooling that must be reached for education to be effective—and there are credit constraints that preclude borrowing to finance education, then universally proportional growth is no longer inevitable: the possibility arises that poor families may be caught in a poverty trap.[3]

To illustrate this, consider the following stripped-down version of Galor and Zeira's (1993) widely cited model. Suppose that investment in human capital is ineffective below some minimal threshold level s. Above this level, when $s_{it+1} > s$, income increases linearly with schooling $y_{it+1} = As_{it+1}$; but below it, when $s_{it+1} < s$, a subsistence income level y is earned, $y_{it+1} = y_{sub}$. Then parents either invest at least the minimal level of schooling s, achieving the utility level given by (5.4); or they do not invest in schooling at all and achieve utility

$$U_{it}^0 = y_{it}^{1-\sigma}/(1 - \sigma) + \delta y_{sub}^{1-\sigma}/(1 - \sigma). \tag{5.5}$$

Comparing (5.4) and (5.5) we find that there is a threshold income level $y > y_{sub}$ such that only parents with income above this threshold invest in schooling. If there is initially a positive mass of families with income below this threshold, then a poverty trap will form: they and their descendants will never invest in schooling and forever remain poor; income growth occurs only among rich families, and initial income differences are amplified over time.

When this is the case, the growth implications of income redistribution vary with the stage of development. When in early stages of economic development the average level of income lies below the threshold level y, then some concentration of effort is required to achieve growth, and excessive redistribution of income will retard progress. Conversely, at later stages, when average income exceeds the threshold level, redistribution can promote growth, as only households with income in excess of the threshold grow at the rate $A\omega$ while the remaining households stagnate at the subsistence level. A redistribution of income that raises all families above the threshold income results in *all* incomes growing at the same rate $A\omega$, thus increasing aggregate growth.[4]

Human-Capital Externalities

Economywide spillovers from education provide yet another rationale for government intervention. Allowing a positive externality from the average level of human capital, we write

$$y_{it} = As_{it}^{\alpha}S_t^{\beta}, \tag{5.6}$$

where $0 < \alpha \leq 1$ and $\beta < 1$, and $S_t = \int s_{it}\, dF_t(y)$ is the average level of human capital in cohort t. Assuming, for simplicity, logarithmic preferences,

$$U(c_{it}, y_{it+1}) = \log(c_{it}) + \delta \log(y_{it+1}), \tag{5.7}$$

parent i invests a fixed proportion of income $\zeta = \alpha\delta/(1 + \alpha\delta)$ in her child's schooling, so that $s_{it+1} = \zeta y_{it}$, and the average level of human capital in the next period is $S_{t+1} = \zeta Y_t$. Transitional income dynamics are then given by $y_{it+1} = A\zeta^{\alpha+\beta}y_{it}^{\alpha}Y_t^{\beta}$, and convergence of average income to a steady state depends on scale effects. If $\alpha < 1$, then all incomes converge to the mean over time, in which case, if $\alpha + \beta < 1$, average income converges to $Y_{\infty} = (A\zeta^{\alpha+\beta})^{1/(1-\alpha-\beta)}$; if $\alpha + \beta = 1$, the growth rate of average income converges to $A\zeta$ and income levels become infinitely large; and if $\alpha + \beta > 1$, the growth rate diverges and becomes infinitely large over time. Finally, if $\alpha = 1$, all household incomes within a cohort grow at the same rate, and the growth rate converges or diverges depending on whether $\beta = 0$ or $\beta > 0$.

When schooling generates a positive externality, private education results in underinvestment in schooling, from a social standpoint. A marginal increase in schooling investment by all households, at the expense of current consumption, would make them all better off. This market failure can be addressed by subsidizing private education[5] or through public education.

Differences in Abilities

The preceding analysis ignored differences in abilities across individuals, so that investment in education was the sole source of income heterogeneity. We now incorporate differences in ability in the model, in the same manner as in chapter 4, assuming that human-capital accumulation is the combined result of formal schooling and direct parental input.[6]

Allowing for either concavity or linearity of the production function and disregarding external effects, we write

$$y_{it} = Aa_{it}s_{it}^{\alpha}, \tag{5.8}$$

where, as before, $0 < \alpha \leq 1$, A is assumed large enough to generate positive growth, and a_{it} designates the individual ability of parent i in period t. The parameter α is the elasticity of income with respect to schooling: the smaller its value, the greater the decline in the marginal productivity of schooling when the level of schooling increases; when $\alpha = 1$, the marginal productivity of schooling is constant across education levels. Initial abilities a_{i0} are exogenously given, and in subsequent periods they are determined by the combined effect of parental ability and a random disturbance term b_{it}:

$$a_{it} = a_{it-1}^{\gamma}b_{it}^{1-\gamma}, \tag{5.9}$$

where $0 \leq \gamma < 1$ measures the relative importance of parental input.[7]

We posit a logarithmic utility function, as in (5.7), and assume that parents know the abilities of their children and seek to maximize their expected utility,

$$EU(c_{it}, y_{it+1}) = \ln(c_{it}) + \delta E \ln(y_{it+1}) = \ln(c_{it}) + \delta E \ln(Aa_{it+1}s_{it+1}^{\alpha}), \tag{5.10}$$

subject to the budget constraint (5.2). The chosen level of private investment in schooling is then the same fixed proportion of income ζ as before, $s_{it+1} = \zeta y_{it}$, and the transitional income dynamics are given by

$$y_{it} = A\zeta^{\alpha}a_{it-1}^{\gamma}b_{it}^{1-\gamma}y_{it-1}^{\alpha}. \tag{5.11}$$

Variation in parental income, transmitted by proportional investment in human capital, is augmented by the partial transmission of parental ability, which is positively correlated with parental ability and partially offset by the random disturbance term.

With additional assumptions specifying the distribution of income and abilities, detailed in the appendix to this chapter, we can track the evolution of abilities and incomes over time and characterize the asymptotic behavior of the economy under two alternative assumptions. Assuming a convex, decreasing returns-to-scale technology ($\alpha < 1$), we obtain a variation of the standard Solow growth model in which the economy converges to a steady-state level of output and growth in the steady state derives only from exogenous increases in the technology parameter A. If the production technology is linear ($\alpha = 1$), we obtain an endogenous growth model in which the economy converges to a steady-state rate of growth. In this case, the marginal productivity of education does not vary with the level of investment in education; this point will be relevant when we compare long-run growth under private and public schooling.

Income Dynamics under Public Schooling

With imperfect access to credit markets, under private education the rich invest more in educating their children than the poor, which inhibits intergenerational income mobility and may perpetuate and even amplify initial inequality. Public education is an instrument of upward mobility for children from poorer backgrounds and a force working to reduce income inequality. Loury (1981) showed that such redistribution could also raise total output. However, this may not always be the case. While public education raises the schooling level of the poor, it may lower the schooling level of the rich compared to private education. The net effect on total output is not necessarily positive.

Consider a pure public system of education that provides all children in each period with the same amount of (free) education and is fully financed by a proportional income tax. Let τ_t denotes the tax rate in period t. Consumption in period t then equals

$$c_{it} = (1 - \tau_t)y_{it}. \tag{5.12}$$

Assuming that the budget is balanced in each period and all tax proceeds are used to finance a uniform level of public schooling, education spending per student in period t is

$$s_{it+1} = \tau_t Y_t. \tag{5.13}$$

We continue to assume that production takes the form $y_{it} = A a_{it} s_{it}^{\alpha}$ and utility is logarithmic in consumption and in next-generation income and to retain our assumptions regarding the initial distribution of abilities and incomes and the subsequent formation of abilities. Uniform spending on education implies that ability differences are the sole source of income heterogeneity across families (after the initial period). Parent i's expected utility in period t equals, after substitution,

$$EU_{it} = \ln[(1 - \tau_t)y_{it}] + \delta E \ln[a_{it+1}(\tau_t Y_t)^{\alpha}], \tag{5.14}$$

and utility maximization implies that all voters in all periods prefer the same tax rate:

$$\tau^* = \alpha\delta/(1 + \alpha\delta) \equiv \zeta. \tag{5.15}$$

This is then the politically chosen tax rate in each period, and it is equal to the proportion of income ζ that individual households spend on schooling under a private education system. Logarithmic utility implies that the overall share of education spending in total income is the same under both regimes, though of course the distribution of education spending is different.

As in the case of private education, additional assumptions specifying the distribution of income and abilities allow us to track the evolution of abilities and incomes over time under public education and to compare the steady states it generates to those generated by private education. We summarize here the results of this comparison with regard to income levels and growth rates, inequality, intergenerational mobility, and popular support, leaving the details of the analysis to the appendix to this chapter.

Income and Growth   The efficiency advantage of public education is greater as the elasticity of schooling in production α is smaller and the intergenerational transmission of abilities γ is weaker. When the production elasticity of schooling is small, its marginal productivity for poor households with low levels of schooling is much greater than for rich households with high levels of schooling. Hence, there is a larger positive effect on growth from moving education resources from the rich to the poor, through public education. This effect is countervailed by a strong intergenerational transmission of ability—large γ—which increases the marginal productivity of schooling for the rich. Thus when the production elasticity of schooling is small and direct parental input has little effect on the accumulation of human capital, the relative efficiency gain from public schooling is greatest.[8] This highlights the importance of beginning public education at an early age and thus reducing the relative importance of parental input, which is consistent with empirical evidence on the greater relative importance of education in the early grades, reviewed in chapter 3. It also suggests that the efficiency advantage of public education may be greatest in periods of skill-biased technological change that generally increase the marginal productivity of education.

Inequality   Income is less dispersed under public schooling than under private schooling (as measured by the variance of the logarithm of income) and has a higher ratio of median to mean income.[9] This stems from the redistributive property of public education, which provides a uniform level of schooling while taxing the rich more than the poor. With constant returns to scale ($\alpha = 1$), inequality increases without bound under private schooling, while under public schooling it remains constant.

Intergenerational Mobility   Comparing the intergenerational correlation of income between parent and child in the steady state under public and private education regimes, we obtain the expected result that public education brings about greater intergenerational mobility. Public education helps poor families overcome credit constraints, thus breaking the link between parental income and the level of a child's education. However, it does not eliminate the effect of parental input on income: even under public education there exists a positive intergenerational correlation of incomes. As many studies have shown, the socioeconomic status of parents continues to exhibit a significant affect on the education and income of their children—despite the prevalence of public schooling (see chapter 3).

Public Support   Comparing the utility of individual parents from public and private schooling, we find that—in the context of this simple model—voters with below-average income support public education while those with incomes above the mean prefer private education.[10] Hence, popular support for public education hinges on the political power of low-income voters. If all households carry equal weight in the political process, the decisive voter household earns median income, which is generally far below the mean, indicating that public education should command a substantial majority. However, if the political process excludes the poorest individuals or accords them less than proportional influence, public education may not gain sufficient support. We expand on this below.

Other factors that influence the comparison between public and private education can be similarly incorporated in dynamic models of education and growth. Positive externalities that derive from the average level of human capital in a cohort add to the relative efficiency of public education. Glomm and Ravikumar (1992) explicitly compare voters' preferences for public education in a growth model with human-capital externalities, showing that positive externalities increase the efficiency of public education in promoting growth and its popularity among voters. Saint-Paul and Verdier (1993) consider a voting model of public education with externalities where they assume that a child's level of human capital depends on her parent's human capital as well as on the amount of public investment in education; this feature implies that the poor prefer higher tax rates than the rich. Eckstein and Zilcha (1994) show that existence of human-capital externalities implies that imposing some minimal amount of public education on a regime of private education is Pareto improving and leads to faster growth.

Public education is associated with inefficiencies stemming from the excess burden of the taxes that finance public schooling, which may have a negative effect on the supply of labor, and thus both inhibit growth and diminish popular support for public education. Perotti (1993) considers these issues in a dynamic setting. Gradstein and Justman (1997), incorporating both positive externalities and the excess burden of taxation, show that for an intermediate range of parameters the choice of a democratic majority between private and public education systems is also the choice that promotes stronger growth.

An important methodological extension developed by Bénabou (1996b, 2000) considers the relationship between education, growth, and distribution in the context of a model in which individuals derive utility not only from their children, as we assume here, but from the incomes of all their descendants. These studies incorporate externalities or agglomeration effects as well as credit constraints and find that although public education slows growth in the short run, in the long run its growth performance is superior to that of private education. This leads to the conclusion that individuals will prefer a public education system if they are sufficiently forward looking.

Public Education and Democracy

Historians of education generally view mass education as a by-product of democratization. In the course of modern economic growth, the boundaries of political participation expand to include voters from the lower ranks of society. This process has been described as the combined outcome of different forces acting with varying strength in different contexts. Acemoglu and Robinson (2000) stipulate two income classes, rich and poor, and assume that the rich, with whom all political power initially rests, extend it to (some of) the poor to ward off the threat of violent upheaval and expropriation. Extending the franchise effectively commits the economy to redistributive policies that offer the poor the prospect of sustained future benefits. Education, though not the focal point of their paper, is an example of such a redistributive program. A related explanation argues that as the incomes of the lower classes rise, their interests grow more closely aligned to those of the already enfranchised upper classes, while the cost of their exclusion from the political process also rises (Justman and Gradstein, 1999). Other explanations center on the lesser inclination of the poor to participate in the political process (Ades and Verdier, 1996; Justman and Gradstein, 1999). There are fixed costs associated with informed, active participation, which the rich and the educated bear more readily than the poor: the consumption value of political participation, the "warm glow" of good citizenship, is a luxury good that ranks below basic needs.[11] As incomes grow, an increasing fraction of the population is prepared to bear the costs of political participation. When political participation expands sufficiently, the majority of enfranchised voters support public education. This process is described graphically in figure 5.1 and analytically in appendix 5.2.

In Britain, the extension of the political franchise was drawn out over a century in successive acts of electoral reform that relaxed the legal economic requirements for political participation, each reform coopting the upper echelons of the disenfranchised. The emergence and subsequent expansion of public education came about as an outgrowth of these political developments, as the newly enfranchised lower classes used their newly acquired political power to enact social policies that served their needs.[12] Of course, public education found broad support also among the upper classes, many of whom appreciated the political importance of educating the newly enfranchised lower classes.[13] Empirical analysis of contemporary evidence similarly demonstrates the

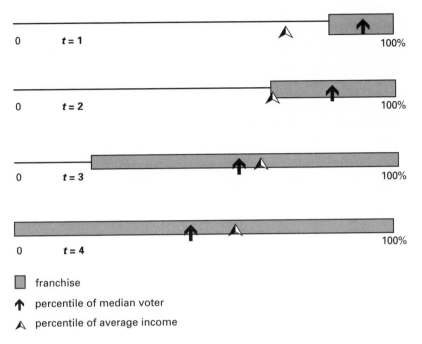

Figure 5.1
Dynamics of enfranchisement and inequality

fiscal consequences of easing formal voting restrictions (e.g., Husted and Kenny, 1997). And in related work, Tavares and Wacziarg (2001) show that political rights—taken as a proxy for democracy—enhance the accumulation of human capital. However, to the best of our knowledge the effect of democratization, directly measured, on the extent of public involvement in education has yet to be analyzed statistically.

Bourguignon and Verdier (2000) and Galor and Moav (2001) advance an alternative approach that views democratization primarily as an outgrowth of wider education. In their view, the enfranchised rich subsidize the education of the poor because of the economic benefits it holds out, which outweigh the anticipated dilution of their political power. Galor and Moav describe these benefits as deriving from positive externalities through which the income of the rich depends on the fraction of educated individuals, externalities that, they argue, increased as a result of the Industrial Revolution. This approach sees subsidization of education as the driving force behind democratization, rather than its outgrowth. While both approaches recognize that

democratization and larger public involvement in education often go
hand in hand, they differ with regard to cause and effect.

Conclusions

The intertemporal framework presented in this chapter illustrates the
long-term effects of education on average income levels, growth rates,
income inequality, and intergenerational mobility. Public education
provides a uniform level of schooling, which removes the credit constraints that limit the private options of the less affluent; thus it reduces
inequality within cohorts and increases intergenerational mobility.
Its effect on future output is not clear-cut and depends on intergenerational transmission of abilities and on the decline in the marginal productivity of schooling when the level of schooling increases.
The weaker the correlation between the abilities of parents and their
children, and the greater the decline in the marginal productivity of
education as the level of schooling rises, the greater the advantage of
public education in promoting aggregate growth. One interpretation
of these findings is that public education is more likely to enhance
long-run output when introduced at a young age, when parental influence on the child's development is relatively small, and in periods of
skill-biased technological change, which increases productivity differences between more and less skilled individuals. However, irrespective
of these output effects, economically less advantaged households invariably benefit from public education, achieving greater welfare
than under private education. This explains why, historically, moves
toward public education were typically made following large waves
of democratization that enhanced the political power of the lower
classes.

Appendix 5.1   Dynamics of the Income Distribution

Distributional Assumptions
Specific assumptions on the distribution of initial incomes and abilities
allow explicit characterization of the income distribution in each period under both private and public education regimes. We assume that
$\ln(a_{i0})$ is distributed normally with zero mean and variance ψ_0^2 and
$\ln(y_{i0})$ is distributed normally with mean μ_0 and variance σ_0^2 and denote by $\theta_0 \geq 0$ the nonnegative covariance between (the logarithms
of) initial incomes and abilities, $\text{Cov}[\ln(y_{i0}), \ln(a_{i0})]$. We further assume

that the disturbance terms b_{it} are distributed lognormally with zero mean and variance ε^2, identically and independently within each cohort and across generations, and that they are uncorrelated with the logarithms of initial abilities and incomes, $\text{Cov}[\ln(a_{i0}), \ln(b_{it})] = \text{Cov}[\ln(y_{i0}), \ln(b_{it})] = 0$.

These assumptions, along with the assumptions on the production technology and on ability formation in the body of the chapter, imply that future distributions of ability and income are also lognormal under both private and public education regimes. Then $\ln(a_{it})$ has zero mean, and (5.9) implies that its variance ψ_t^2 follows the recursive equation[14]

$$\psi_t^2 = \gamma^2 \psi_{t-1}^2 + (1-\gamma)^2 \varepsilon^2, \tag{5.16}$$

which goes to $\psi_\infty^2 = (1-\gamma)^2 \varepsilon^2 / (1-\gamma^2)$ as t goes to infinity. Letting μ_t and σ_t^2 denote the mean and variance of $\ln(y_{it})$, mean income in period t is given by $Y_t = \exp(\mu_t + \sigma_t^2/2)$; the logarithm of the economy's growth rate is defined by $g_t = \ln(Y_t/Y_{t-1})$; and the intergenerational correlation coefficient of income is defined by $\rho_t = \text{cov}[\ln(y_{it}), \ln(y_{it-1})]/(\sigma_t \sigma_{t-1})$.

Intertemporal Evolution

Considering first *private education*, we obtain μ_t, σ_t^2 and ρ_t from equation (5.11), where θ_t, the covariance of $\ln(y_{it})$ and $\ln(a_{it})$, is calculated recursively from[15]

$$\theta_t = \psi_t^2 + \alpha\gamma\theta_{t-1}, \tag{5.17}$$

and the growth rate is then calculated as the difference in the logarithms of mean income between the current and preceding periods. This determines the intertemporal evolution of the economy. The parameters of the distribution of output in the steady state, when $\alpha < 1$ and there is convergence to a steady-state output, are derived by setting $\mu_t = \mu_{t-1}$ and $\sigma_t^2 = \sigma_{t-1}^2$ and noting that θ_t goes to $\psi_\infty^2/(1-\alpha\gamma)$ as t goes to infinity; when $\alpha = 1$, only the growth rate converges to a steady state. These values are presented in the left-hand column of table 5.1.

Similarly, for *public education*, the distribution of income in each generation is derived by substituting (5.13) in (5.8), where the tax rate is given by (5.15) to obtain

$$y_{it} = Aa_{it}(\zeta Y_t)^\alpha.$$

Table 5.1
Income distribution under private and public education: Summary of results

Private Education	Public Education
$\mu_t = \ln(A\zeta^\alpha) + \alpha\mu_{t-1}$	$\mu_t^* = \ln(A\zeta^\alpha) + \alpha\mu_{t-1}^* + \frac{\alpha}{2}\sigma_{t-1}^{*\,2}$
$\sigma_t^2 = \psi_t^2 + \alpha^2\sigma_{t-1}^2 + 2\alpha\gamma\theta_{t-1}$	$\sigma_t^* = \psi_t^2$
$\rho_t = (\alpha\sigma_{t-1}^2 + \gamma\theta_{t-1})/(\sigma_t\sigma_{t-1})$	$\rho_t^* = \gamma\psi_{t-1}/\psi_t$
$g_t = \mu_t - \mu_{t-1} + \frac{1}{2}[\sigma_t^2 - \sigma_{t-1}^2]$	$g_t^* = \mu_t^* - \mu_{t-1}^*$

Long run, a < 1

$\mu_\infty = \ln(A\zeta^\alpha)/(1-\alpha)$	$\mu_\infty^* = (\ln A\zeta^\alpha + \alpha\psi_\infty^2)/(1-\alpha)$
$\sigma_\infty^2 = \psi_\infty^2\dfrac{1+\alpha\gamma}{(1-\alpha^2)(1-\alpha\gamma)}$	$\sigma_\infty^{*\,2} = \psi_\infty^2$
$\rho_\infty = (\alpha+\gamma)/(1+\alpha\gamma)$	$\rho_\infty^{*\,2} = \gamma$
$\ln Y_\infty = \left\{\ln A\zeta^\alpha + \psi_\infty^2\dfrac{1+\alpha\gamma}{2(1+\alpha)(1-\alpha\gamma)}\right\}\bigg/(1-\alpha)$	$\ln Y_\infty = \left\{\ln A\zeta^\alpha + \dfrac{1+\alpha}{2}\psi_\infty^2\right\}\bigg/(1-\alpha)$

Long run, a = 1

$g_\infty = \ln\dfrac{A\delta}{1+\delta} + \dfrac{1}{2}\varepsilon^2$	$g_\infty^* = \ln\dfrac{A\delta}{1+\delta} + \dfrac{(1-\gamma)^2}{1-\gamma^2}\dfrac{1}{2}\varepsilon^2$

Thus here, too, income is distributed lognormally in each period, and we can recursively derive the parameters of its distribution in each period. The parameters of the distribution in the steady state are obtained similarly to the case of private education. The parameter values for public education are marked with an asterisk and presented in the right-hand column of table 5.1.

Note that under both private and public education, transmission of abilities γ has a negative effect on mean income and inequality in the steady state and a positive effect on the intergenerational correlation of incomes. Combining the two latter effects we find that, through this effect of γ, income inequality and income mobility are positively related, a result that is consistent with Checchi et al.'s (1999) comparison between Italy and the United States, which found both greater inequality and greater mobility in the United States. Moreover, variation in γ also generates a positive long-run association between inequality and mean income. It should be stressed, however, that this is not the causal relation between inequality and growth suggested by several recent studies (e.g., Persson and Tabellini, 1994) but the joint result of variation in a third, structural factor—the intergenerational transmission of abilities.

Comparison between Private and Public Schooling in the Long Run

Steady-State Output ($a < 1$)   Comparing the levels of steady-state output in table 5.1 we have

$$\ln Y_\infty{}^* - \ln Y_\infty = \tfrac{1}{2}\psi_\infty{}^2\{(1 + \alpha) - (1 + \alpha\gamma)/[(1 + \alpha)(1 - \alpha\gamma)]\},$$

which is positive if and only if $\gamma(\alpha + 2) < 1$.

Steady-State Growth Rates ($a = 1$)   Comparing the levels of steady-state growth rates when $\alpha = 1$, we obtain stronger growth under private schooling:

$$g_\infty{}^* - g_\infty = \tfrac{1}{2}\varepsilon^2[(1 - \gamma)^2/(1 - \gamma^2) - 1] < 0$$

as $(1 - \gamma)^2 < 1 - \gamma^2$ for $\gamma < 1$.

Inequality   In the long run, with decreasing returns to scale, inequality in the steady state, as measured by the variance of the logarithm of income, is less under public schooling than under private schooling.

Intergenerational Mobility   With decreasing returns to scale, public education results in less intergenerational correlation in incomes in the steady state than private education, as

$$\rho_\infty{}^* - \rho_\infty = \gamma - (\alpha + \gamma)/(1 + \alpha\gamma) < 0.$$

Appendix 5.2   Political Dynamics

The dynamics of political participation described in figure 5.1 can be derived as follows. Assume that the political franchise is defined by a set income requirement $\hat{y}$ so that only individuals with income larger than $\hat{y}$ vote.[16] In each period, enfranchised individuals vote on the type of education system, private or public, and the system that wins the support of a majority of voters is put into place. Assuming a linear production technology $\alpha = 1$ and lognormal distribution of income as in appendix 5.1, the intertemporal evolution of the parameters of the income distribution under private education is described in table 5.1.

Because the utility differential between public and private education is monotonic in income,[17] the decisive voter in each period will be the median income voter among enfranchised households. Denoting its income y_{dt}, it is defined by

$$F_t(y_{dt}) = F_t(\hat{y}) + \tfrac{1}{2}[1 - F_t(\hat{y})] = F_t(\hat{y}) + \tfrac{1}{2}. \tag{5.18}$$

Assuming that initially the franchise requirement and the distribution of income are such that the decisive voter's income exceeds the mean, $y_{d0} > Y_0$ ($t = 0$ in figure 5.1). This implies that initially a majority of voters prefer a private education regime, and as long as this holds—as long as $F_t(y_{dt}) > F_t(Y_t)$—private education will remain the preferred choice, and there will be no public education. This holds as long as[18]

$$\Phi(\tfrac{1}{2}\sigma_t) - \Phi[(\ln \hat{y} - \mu_t)/\sigma_t] < \tfrac{1}{2}. \tag{5.19}$$

If growth is strong enough, the inequality sign in (5.19) is eventually reversed ($t = 3$ in figure 5.1), at which point there is a decisive coalition of poorer voters who favor public education and impose it on the economy. Then the combined effect of continued growth in incomes and decrease in inequality, achieved through public education, causes further increase in the fraction of enfranchised voters, implying further decline in the income percentile of the decisive voter until universal suffrage is achieved ($t = 4$ in figure 5.1). Thus once public education is adopted it prevails in all future periods.

6   Central versus Local Education Finance

It is one of the happy incidents of the federal system that a single courageous state may, if its citizens choose, serve as a laboratory; and try novel social and economic experiments without risk to the rest of the country.

—Louis D. Brandeis, Dissent in *New State Ice Co. v. Liebmann* (1932)

The choice between local and central financing of education implies a tradeoff between the advantages of local control in achieving a better fit between preferences and spending and the advantages of centralized funding in achieving greater equality of opportunity.

Historically, public involvement in education financing, both in Europe and in the United States, began at the local community level before gravitating to more centralized funding at the national, provincial, or state level. In Europe, national control of education was often an important component of nineteenth-century nation building, promoting the development and assimilation of a common national culture in culturally diverse regions. National governments set unified standards for school hours, curriculum content, teacher accreditation, physical facilities, and education spending across local communities. However, there remain significant differences in the division of financial responsibilities for education between different layers of government even among similar countries.[1] In Belgium, Ireland, the Netherlands, Germany, and Italy, local funding constitutes a small fraction of total spending, whereas in Denmark and the United Kingdom it is a major source of education finance.

In the United States, increased involvement of the states in education finance is a more recent development aimed at reducing inequality in school funding by requiring richer communities to subsidize public education in poorer communities. The California Supreme Court's landmark *Serrano v. Priest* decision, in 1971, was a watershed in this regard that severely limited local variation in education finance across school districts in the state. Many others states followed in California's wake, some responding to similar court decisions in their own supreme courts while others legislated change before it was mandated. These include placing restrictions on the property taxes levied by local school districts to finance education and using categorical and foundation grants to redistribute education resources across districts.[2] This has steadily reduced the share of local revenues in public school spending, which in 1999–2000 accounted for just over 40 percent of elementary and high school spending, less than the share of state funding, which was nearly 50 percent. Yet there remains significant variation among states in this regard. The share of local revenues in public school spending in the contiguous forty-eight states ranges from less than 20 percent of revenues in New Mexico and Vermont to around 60 percent in Illinois and Nevada (National Center for Education Statistics 2002, table 157).

In this chapter, we consider economic models that highlight the tradeoffs implied in the choice between local and central financing of public education and the policy issues that arise in this context. We first describe how differences in demand for education across individuals can result in residential segregation by income. Then assuming that such sorting does indeed occur, we compare different education financing regimes in which central and local authorities interact. The analysis indicates that the choice between central and local funding often involves a tradeoff between aggregate spending on education and its equal distribution.

Demand for Education Quality and Residential Segregation

Residential segregation by income is a common phenomenon largely explained by variation in housing quality within school districts, willingness to pay for local public goods and amenities, and externalities that are positively correlated with income (Nechyba, 2003). Assume that public education is locally financed and there is no private schooling.[3] Then if affluent families desire a higher level of education for their children and are willing to spend more on education than poorer families, the education tax they levy on local properties may deter poor families from moving to the wealthier neighborhood. Moreover, if local public education is financed by proportional taxes on property values, the more affluent families have strong motivation to use zoning laws to place a lower bound on local property values and thus exclude poorer families that might otherwise choose to live in lower-cost housing in the wealthy district and pay less than a proportionate share of education costs. Positive externalities in schooling that are correlated with parental income further reinforce the motivation of the rich to segregate themselves from the poor.

The following simple model of residential segregation follows Tiebout (1956). It abstracts for the moment from real estate values, from school choice, from peer-group effects, and from intrinsic variation in preferences for education. Assume that a population of households comprises two income groups indexed by $i = p, r$—poor households with income y_p, and rich households with income y_r—and assume that the poor are more numerous than the rich. Each household can choose between residing in one of two districts, indexed by $j = a, b$.[4] A household of income group i living in district j derives utility from consumption c_{ij} and from spending on local public schooling s_j. Letting τ_j denote the education tax rate in district j, consumption equals after-tax income: $c_{ij} = (1 - \tau_j)y_i$. Letting Y_j denote the mean income level in district j and assuming that tax revenues are used to provide a uniform quality of public education within each school district, local education quality is $s_j = \tau_j Y_j$. The utility of a household of income group i living in district j is then

$$U(c_{ij}, s_j) = U((1 - \tau_j)y_i, \tau_j Y_j). \tag{6.1}$$

Raising the education tax increases spending on local public schooling but reduces current consumption.

An equilibrium consists of an allocation of all households among the two communities and of tax rates in the two districts, such that (1) no household can improve its lot by changing its district of residence and (2) in each district the tax rate that obtains has the support of the majority of households residing in the district. The equilibrium is stable if after moving a small mass of households from one district to the other, the tax rates approved by the majority in each district generate incentives for these households to return to their original communities.

If the desired tax rate is an increasing monotonic function of household income—which holds, for example, for a CES utility function with an elasticity of substitution less than one—two types of stable equilibria are possible.[5] One type is a segregating equilibrium in which rich and poor reside in separate districts. A necessary and sufficient condition for such an equilibrium to hold is that there is no incentive for the poor to move to the rich district (the rich can have no incentive to migrate). This holds if the disadvantage to the poor of the higher tax rate—and hence lower consumption—in the rich district more than offsets the advantage of its better schools. This type of equilibrium is efficient, as both districts are internally homogeneous and so choose their respective tax rates optimally.[6] This is the essence of the Tiebout analysis: perfect sorting of individuals into homogeneous communities with internally uniform demand for education—or other local publicly provided goods—leads to an efficient allocation of resources.

In the second type of stable equilibrium, district a is a mixed community in which the rich are in the majority, and district b is uniformly poor. In such an equilibrium, decentralized school financing implies that both tax rates and school quality must be higher in the mixed district and that the poor are indifferent between the two districts. To see that such an equilibrium is stable, assume a small number of poor households move to district a, the mixed district. Then the resulting deterioration of the tax base in district a must leave the poor migrants worse off for migrating, causing them to move back. This equilibrium is clearly inefficient compared to a segregating equilibrium, as the poor achieve the same level welfare in both cases but the rich are worse off. The rich majority in district a can achieve a Pareto improvement by subsidizing schooling in district b to induce the poor to move away from district a. This will increase school spending in both districts without raising tax rates.

Fernandez and Rogerson (1996) consider a similar inefficiency in local provision of education in an economy with two districts and three income groups, in which the poor exclusively reside in one district, the rich reside in the other district, and only middle-income households can be found in both districts. In equilibrium, a marginal fiscal transfer from the richer to the poorer district would benefit all, as it would induce a small number of middle-income households to move to the poor community and thus raise mean income in both communities without changing the identity of the decisive voter. This must increase everyone's welfare. Again, the nonsegregating equilibrium is inefficient because the individual household ignores the external effect of its choice of residence on the local tax base and, through it, on the quality of local education.

Bénabou (1993, 1994) obtains similar results from peer-group effects in education. Consider an economy with two districts populated by individuals with different initial endowments of human capital, and assume that the accumulation of human capital that generates next-period income depends both on one's own education and on average education in one's district. If one's own education and the average education of one's peers are complements, then individual residential choices will generate segregation, with those with initial endowments above a certain threshold residing in one district and those below the threshold residing in the other. As in Fernandez and Rogerson (1996), the resulting equilibrium is inefficient, and it is possible to achieve a Pareto improvement by paying some "middling" individuals, with initial endowments just above the threshold, to move from the richer to the poorer district.

Local and Central Education Funding

We next focus our analysis on the interaction between central and local authorities in financing public education, assuming that Tiebout sorting has already segregated the population by income and removed all within-district variation.[7]

Consider a population of households of unit measure, segregated into a fixed number of internally homogeneous school districts of equal size, indexed by j, and denote by Y_j the initial income level of each resident of district j. Utility is derived from consumption and from public education spending per pupil in one's district. Under pure *local finance*, district j imposes a tax rate of τ_j on the income of local residents;[8] school spending per student in the district is then $s_j = \tau_j Y_j$, and consumption equals after-tax income, $c_j = (1 - \tau_j)Y_j$. The chosen tax rate in district j maximizes $U((1 - \tau_j)Y_j, \tau_j Y_j)$ over τ_j. As all district j's residents have the same income, this is the same as choosing the education level s_j to maximize $U(Y_j - s_j, s_j)$, which is formally equivalent to the private education regime analyzed in chapter 4's A Basic Model of Private Education section. Pure local funding of public education results in differences in education spending across jurisdictions that mirror differences that arise under private education. Our assumptions on preferences imply that spending on education is monotonically increasing in district income. In the special case of CES preferences, education spending is a fixed fraction of income, so that the elasticity of education spending with respect to income is unity; under a Stone-Geary specification, it may be greater or smaller than unity.

In the United States, large disparities in education spending under predominantly local funding have been rejected in the courts and in the political arena, leading many states to adopt equalization schemes that transfer funds from rich to poor districts, while constraining education spending in all districts to fall between narrowly defined limits. In the extreme case of pure *central financing*, there is no variation among districts in spending per student,[9] and education is financed by a uniform tax on the residents of all districts, who vote on the level of the tax. Assuming a proportional income tax and denoting its rate by τ, school spending is $s_j = \tau Y$ in all districts, where Y denotes average income in the economy as a whole, and consumption equals after-tax income $c_j = (1 - \tau)Y_j$. Each household chooses its preferred tax rate by maximizing $U((1 - \tau)Y_j, \tau Y)$ over τ, and political equilibrium is defined, as before, as a tax rate τ^* that cannot be defeated by a majority in pairwise comparison with any other tax rate. This is formally equivalent to the case of public schooling analyzed in chapter 4.

Because of the formal similarity between local and central financing on the one hand and private and public education on the other hand, we can apply the analysis of chapter 4 to the comparison between local and central school finance. It shows that centralized education finance reduces inequality in school spending among school districts relative to local finance. It is opposed by districts with above-average schooling, which now must pay more for the same quality of public education, and generally favored by districts with less than average income, which pay less per dollar of schooling, though very poor districts may prefer local finance because they find the centralized tax rate too high. Comparing the implications of central and local education finance for aggregate education spending, we find that they depend on the elasticity of substitution in the utility function. With preferences represented by a CES utility function, an elasticity of substitution greater than one implies that centralized school funding generates more education spending than local funding; and vice versa. In California, total education spending declined after the *Serrano* decision greatly reduced variation in local school spending, indicating an elasticity of substitution less than one (Fernandez and Rogerson, 1999).

Dynamic Implications

Several studies have considered the dynamic implications of central versus local education finance. Bénabou (1996a, 1996b) compares the two in a dynamic growth model with initial regional inequalities and production spillovers. As suggested by the preceding analysis, central education financing reduces income inequality. This works to the relative advantage of centralized education—compared to private schooling—in promoting aggregate growth. Thus Bénabou's dynamic analysis implies that, beyond its short-term effects, centralized schooling promotes growth in the long run by reducing inequality. The more far-sighted voters are in their choice of education regime, the greater the weight they will attach to this long-run advantage of centralized education finance.

Identifying the households in chapter 5 with homogeneous local communities, the dynamic model analyzed in chapter 5 can also be applied to compare local and central school financing as they evolve over time and affect income in the long-run steady state. This analysis departs from Bénabou's in two important respects: it incorporates intergenerational transmission of abilities, absent in Bénabou's analysis, while assuming away the spillover effects that play a crucial role in Bénabou's model. Our analysis indicates that if the production technology is concave and the impact of parental input is sufficiently small, then imposition of uniform centralized schooling increases the average level of income in the long run, compared to local schooling. Under local financing, poor communities face credit constraints generation after generation.[10] Relaxing these constraints through centralized funding brings long-lasting benefits, which can generate stronger long-run growth than local schooling, even when centralized schooling generates less growth in the short run.

Fernandez and Rogerson (1998) calibrate a political economy model of school finance to United States data to assess the dynamic effects of centralized school finance at the state level, incorporating residency choice in their model as well as political choice of the school tax. The segregation that results from pure local financing allows households more efficiently to sort themselves into communities according to their demand for education quality, compared to a centralized regime. However, centralized school finance is more effective in reducing income inequality, which has a positive effect on long-run growth, as in Bénabou's model. While it is not possible to determine, in general, which of these effects is stronger, Fernandez and Rogerson's calibration indicates that the centralized system results in higher average income and greater social welfare in the long run than local financing.

Mixed Modes of Education Financing

Typically, public funding of education is neither purely local nor purely central but combines local and central funding sources in different ways.[11] Often, there is central subsidization of specific costs, such as busing or special education, according to specific formulae. Here we focus initially on a different form of mixed finance—"foundation grant" regimes in which the central government funds a minimal level of education spending from centrally levied taxes, which local jurisdictions may choose to supplement. This system roughly corresponds to financing schemes used in several European countries, such as Germany, and its structure reflects the basic rationale of finance equalization schemes that some states have recently implemented in the United States. In the following sections, we describe how foundation grants work and compare them to pure local and central financing regimes before considering the more complex "power equalization" financing methods with which some states are experimenting.

Foundation Grants

Under a foundation-grant regime, the central government funds a minimal level of education spending from centrally levied taxes, which local jurisdictions may then choose to supplement. As before, we assume that households derive utility from consumption and education spending. We let τ denote the education-tax rate levied by the central government, denote by τ_j the local tax rate for funding supplemental education spending, and let $z_j = \tau_j Y_j$ denote the additional amount of education spending in district j, where $0 \leq z_j \leq (1 - \tau)Y_j$. The parental budget constraint is then

$$c_j + z_j = (1 - \tau)Y_j, \tag{6.2}$$

and total per-student education spending in district j equals

$$s_j = \tau Y + z_j. \tag{6.3}$$

The education tax rates at both the central and local levels are determined by voting: first at the central level to determine the size of the foundation grant and then in each district to decide on the amount of supplemental spending. An equilibrium consists of a central education tax that cannot be defeated by a majority of all voters against any alternative rate and supplementary education spending levels in the local districts, which the (identical) residents of each district find optimal, given the size of the foundation grant.

We solve the model recursively, first characterizing the optimal supplementary purchase of schooling in district j taking the central education tax rate τ as given.[12] Maximization of the utility function with respect to z_j yields either

$$-U_c((1-\tau)Y_j, \tau Y) + U_s((1-\tau)Y_j, \tau Y) \leq 0, \tag{6.4a}$$

in which case district j chooses not to supplement the foundation grant from its own resources, or, there is a positive level of local spending z_j that satisfies

$$-U_c((1-\tau)Y_j - z_j, \tau Y + z_j) + U_s((1-\tau)Y_j - z_j, \tau Y + z_j) = 0. \tag{6.4b}$$

It follows that there is a threshold level of local income, such that districts with income below the threshold do not supplement the foundation grant. Above the threshold, local supplementary spending on education is an increasing function of local income, as education is a normal good, spending on which increases with income, and a decreasing function of the central tax rate, as central and local spending on education are substitutes. In the CES case, for example, we have

$$z_j = \mathrm{Max}\{0, [(1-\tau)Y_j - \delta^{-\sigma}\tau Y]/(1+\delta^{-\sigma})\}. \tag{6.5}$$

Next, solving the model for the central tax rate τ, we first characterize the preferred tax rate of a household in district j, maximizing its utility with respect to τ while anticipating the local supplement z_j described by (6.4). The first-order condition implies that either

$$-Y_j U_c(Y_j - z_j, z_j) + Y U_s(Y_j - z_j, z_j) \leq 0, \tag{6.6a}$$

in which case households in district j prefer a zero central tax rate, opting to fund education spending locally and dispense with foundation grants, or there is a positive central tax rate τ implicitly determined by

$$-Y_j U_c((1-\tau)Y_j - z_j, \tau Y + z_j) + Y U_s((1-\tau)Y_j - z_j, \tau Y + z_j) = 0, \tag{6.6b}$$

which households in district j prefer to any other tax rate. Combining (6.4) and (6.6) reveals that each district prefers to rely exclusively on either central or local funding:[13] as state and local spending are perfect substitutes, each district chooses the type of funding with the lower tax price. For households in districts with income above the mean, $Y_j > Y$, local funding is cheaper than central funding, and hence they prefer a zero central tax rate and would rather fund public schooling solely from local taxes.[14] The opposite applies to households in districts with less than average income: they prefer that the foundation grant fund their entire demand for public education.

Note that the preferences of all voters over the central tax rate are single peaked. In districts with less than average income, where voters would rather not fund education locally, the induced utility function is exactly the same as in chapter 4's Public Schooling section, where single-peakedness was shown to hold. In contrast, for voters from districts with above-average income, who would rather fund all their education locally, the envelope theorem together with the concavity of the utility function imply single-peakedness.[15] This implies that there exists a political equilibrium in which the median preferred tax rate prevails over all other tax rates,[16] and given the assumed skewness of the distribution of income, which implies that a majority of voters have less than average income and therefore prefer to fund education centrally, the chosen level of the foundation grant is strictly positive.

The preferred foundation grant and locally funded supplementary spending are illustrated in figure 6.1, where S_1 describes the desired level of school spending in district j as a function of district income Y_j under pure local financing, and S_2 describes the desired level of spending under pure central financing. The tax price of education spending in a centralized regime is Y_j/Y, which is increasing in income, and S_1 and S_2 intersect where the tax price is the same under both regimes, at $Y_j = Y$. Figure 6.1 assumes that the desired level of spending is increasing in income under central funding, implying that when income rises the positive effect of the income effect on school spending outweighs the negative effect of the increase in the tax price; for a CES utility function, this corresponds to an elasticity of substitution less than one. Under a foundation grant system, the decisive household, with income Y_d, sets the foundation grant equal to its desired level of schooling under a pure central regime.[17] The level of total demand for schooling in district j is then given by the thick line marked S_3. The tax price of supplemental education is one, and so districts with income below $\underline{Y}$ do not supplement the foundation grant. Districts with income between $\underline{Y}$ and average income Y spend more on schooling under a foundation grant regime than under pure local funding—because the foundation grant leaves them with more disposable income while the marginal tax price equals one under both

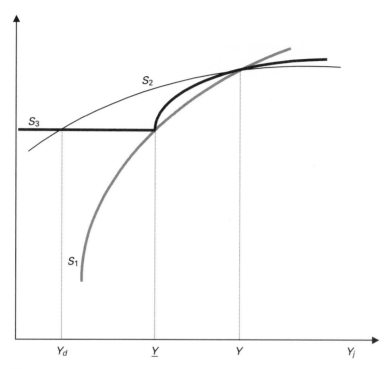

Figure 6.1
Education spending as a function of local income and the type of funding regime

regimes[18]—but less than under pure central financing in which they pay the same for the foundation level of schooling but face a lower tax price. The converse holds for districts with above-average income: under a foundation-grant regime they spend less than under pure local financing because they have less disposable income but more than under pure central financing where they face a higher tax price.

The coalitions that determine the central tax depend strongly on the shape of the utility function. To fix ideas, assume a CES utility function, for which local funding in district j is given by (6.5), and assume initially an elasticity of substitution less than one. Districts with above-average income always prefer a zero foundation grant, as they prefer funding all education locally and form a political alignment with low-income districts, which prefer a smaller foundation grant than middle-income households. The coalitions that form in this case are thus not rich versus poor, but "ends against the middle," with the income of the decisive district Y_d implicitly determined by[19]

$$1 - F(Y) + F(Y_d) = \tfrac{1}{2}. \tag{6.7}$$

As before, F denotes the cumulative distribution function of income. Equation (6.7) implies that $F(Y_d) < \tfrac{1}{2}$ so that the decisive district earns less than median income, $Y_d < Y_m$; and the foundation tax rate, which equals $\tau_f = \delta/[(Y_d/Y)^{\sigma-1}\delta^{1-\sigma} + \delta]$, is less than the equilibrium tax rate τ^* under pure central funding.

When the elasticity of substitution σ is greater than one, the preferred tax rate is a monotonically decreasing function of local income. Therefore, in political equilibrium, the decisive voter resides in a district with median income Y_m, as in the case of pure central schooling, and the tax rate is the same: $\tau_f = \tau^* = \delta/[(Y_m/Y)^{\sigma-1}\delta^{1-\sigma} + \delta]$. Again, as in the case of σ less than one, there is an income threshold above which districts supplement the foundation grant with local funding. When the elasticity of substitution equals one (the logarithmic case), all districts with less than average income prefer the same tax rate, which is the same rate as under pure central funding, $\tau_f = \tau^* = \delta/(1+\delta)$. As they are in the majority, this is the political equilibrium, and districts with income above a certain threshold supplement the foundation grant with local funding.

Comparing Foundation Grants to Pure Central or Local Funding

Local funding is efficient in matching spending levels to individual preferences, while central funding promotes greater equality in education spending. Foundation grants are a compromise between the two. We compare the three regimes with regard to their effect on growth, equality, welfare, and political support.

Inequality in Education Spending The comparison of foundation grants to pure central funding with regard to equality in the distribution of education spending is straightfoward. Pure central funding eliminates all differences in public spending, while foundation-grant regimes leave some variation, provided the grant is not so large as fully to satisfy demand for education in all districts. Moreover, under fairly general assumptions, inequality in education spending decreases with the size of the foundation grant.[20] As pure local financing can be viewed as a special case of a foundation grant with a zero central tax, it induces larger differences in education spending than a foundation-grant regime (with a positive grant).

Card and Payne's (2002) comprehensive study of local education spending in the United States supports these conclusions. They find that more active involvement of the state in education financing is associated not only with greater equality in spending but also in education outcomes, increasing the fraction of disadvantaged students who take the SAT and reducing the difference in SAT scores between children of highly educated and poorly educated parents. Wyckoff (1992) documents more specifically the reduction in spending variation following court decisions on equalization of spending across districts. Murray et al. (1998) concur but find that most of the equalization in school spending has occurred between, rather than within, states.

Total Education Spending First, comparing foundation-grant regimes to pure central funding, we find from the preceding analysis that when the preferred tax rate is a nondecreasing function of income (in the CES case, when the elasticity of substitution is greater than or equal to one), then the decisive voter is the same in both cases, and the foundation grant equals total spending under pure central funding. Hence, if there is some heterogeneity in income among districts, supplemental spending by higher-income districts implies that total spending is higher under the foundation-grant regime.

However, when the preferred tax rate is a decreasing function of income (in the CES case, when the elasticity of substitution is less than one), the formation of a coalition of "ends against the middle" results in a lower central tax rate under a foundation-grant regime, and the net effect on total spending is ambiguous. Fernandez and Rogerson (1999) calibrate a simple theoretical model, using a CES specification with $\sigma < 1$. Their findings indicate that moving to a pure state system of education finance should precipitate a decline of between 8 percent and 13 percent in aggregate spending on education, depending on the precise value of the elasticity of substitution. Fernandez and Rogerson (1999) and Silva and Sonstelie (1995) find support for this conclusion in the experience of California, where education finance reform that moved the state from a mixed system to something close to pure central funding caused a drop of 10 percent in education spending.

Comparing a foundation-grant system to pure local financing, we find that introducing a foundation grant increases spending for the education of low-income districts (districts with income below $\underline{Y}$ in figure 6.1) while lowering it for higher-income districts, as they now have less disposable income from which to supplement the foundation grant. The net effect is generally ambiguous, but in the special case of logarithmic utility, the amount of education spending under local financing is the same as the foundation grant, $\delta Y/(1 + \delta)$, implying that total spending on education spending is higher under the foundation-grant regime. Fernandez and Rogerson (2003) calibrate a model such as this to United States data using different CES specifications. Their results indicate that the mixed system typically generates a higher level of education spending than pure local finance. Card and Payne (2002) present an empirical analysis of the effects of state aid on total education spending, using school-district data in the United States. They find that each additional dollar of state aid increases total spending by 30 to 65 cents.

Popular Support   Because local financing is a special case of a mixed system with a foundation grant and central tax rate equal to zero, the majority choice of a positive central tax proves, by revealed preference, that it benefits a majority of voters. Epple and Romano (1996b) show that a foundation-grant regime is also preferred by a majority of households to pure central schooling.[21] To see this, denote by τ^* the education tax rate chosen under pure central funding. Then holding it constant and allowing districts to supplement it with additional local spending must be a Pareto improvement, as districts that choose to do so must be better off while others are no worse off. As the equilibrium tax rate under a foundation-grant regime τ_f has the support of a majority of voters against any alternative, including τ^* with supplemental spending, it must be preferred by a majority to pure central funding.

Welfare Comparison   In the absence of any external effects, pure local funding of education spending, which allows individual districts to tailor education spending to local preferences, is Pareto efficient. By the same token, both pure central funding and a foundation-grant regime are inefficient because they mandate a uniform level of education spending for districts with diverse preferences. Of course, this ignores other important considerations, such as the intrinsic value that people place on equality of opportunity. Fernandez and Rogerson (2003) simulate a utilitarian social welfare function and find that for reasonable parameter values a foundation-grant regime is welfare-superior to other regimes.

Other Power-Equalization Schemes

The United States has seen increased experimentation with education financing schemes that combine state and local funding in new ways to achieve a more equitable distribution of education spending while maintaining some measure of local choice to reflect local preferences. In addition to the foundation grants described above, states have adopted "power-equalization" schemes that typically specify a uniform tax base across districts while allowing differences in tax rates. This results in the state effectively taxing districts with high local spending on education at a higher rate than districts with low education spending, which reduces differences in education spending across districts. California is an extreme case in this regard, guaranteeing nearly equal education spending across districts regardless of how much revenue is raised in the district through education taxes.

Fernandez and Rogerson (1998, 2003) use calibrations to compare several such schemes and find that a power-equalization scheme with recapture (PER) is welfare-superior to other considered schemes. Under such a scheme, all households first vote on a common statewide tax base B, and then each district chooses its local tax rate τ_j. The amount of education spending in district j equals

$$s_j = \tau_j B, \tag{6.8}$$

and a statewide tax rate of τ_B is levied to balance the budget. If all districts are of equal size, Y_j is the actual tax base in district j, and Y is the average tax base in the state, then τ_B is defined by

$$\tau_B Y = \Sigma_j \tau_j (B - Y_j). \tag{6.9}$$

The individual budget constraint for households residing in district j then implies that

$$c_j = (1 - \tau_B - \tau_j)Y_j. \tag{6.10}$$

In contrast to foundation-grant regimes, PER does not guarantee a minimal level of education spending but does reduce variability in education spending across districts.

Comparing different funding regimes, Fernandez and Rogerson (2003) find substantial differences among them, both in terms of total education spending and of the inequality in spending that they generate, sometimes presenting tradeoffs between these two objectives. Fernandez and Rogerson (2003) show—analytically in some cases, by calibration in others—that PER results in higher aggregate education spending than either local or state funding schemes; and in lower variability across districts than foundation grants. Using a utilitarian welfare criterion, they also establish that PER yields a higher level of welfare than any alternative scheme and is more likely to constitute the preferred choice of a majority of voters, except when the elasticity of substitution is close enough to one, in which case a foundation-grant regime is welfare-superior to PER.

Conclusions

In this chapter we examined the interaction between central and local funding of public education. Local education finance matches local spending to local preferences but may lead to large discrepancies in education spending across districts, through residential segregation by income. Large differences in the quality of education between wealthy and poorer districts undermine the principle of equal opportunity, and the inequality they generate may have significant welfare costs for society as a whole.

A pure centralized regime of education funding results in equal spending but is likely to be inefficient in a world where demand for education quality differs across communities. Consequently, many systems of education finance combine local and central funding that reconcile in some measure the conflicting objectives of equity and efficiency, and they may therefore be preferred to either purely local or central funding. Foundation-grant regimes guarantee all districts a minimum level of centrally funded spending, which individual districts may then supplement. Power-equalization regimes with recapture (PER) set a common tax base for all districts while allowing each to set its own tax rate, effectively taxing districts that spend more on education at a higher rate than districts that spend less. Numerical simulation indicates that both foundation-grant and PER regimes are welfare-superior to either pure regime for a large range of parameter values, achieving higher aggregate utility and greater popular support. The limited empirical analysis on these issues offers tentative support to the hypothesis that combining central and local funding can increase overall education spending while reducing variation in education quality. But more research is needed to better understand the politics and welfare implications of different architectures of education finance.

7   Mixed Regimes of Public and Private Schooling

The method will be to allow for each of those children ten shillings a year for the expense of schooling, for six years each, which will give them six months schooling each year and half a crown a year for paper and spelling books.

—Thomas Paine, *The Rights of Man*, Part 2, "Ways and Means of Improving the Condition of Europe" (1984/1792)

In the preceding chapters we considered pure forms of public and private education. In this chapter and the following we consider the coexistence of and interaction between public and private education in two different contexts. In the next chapter we consider an education system that offers parents a choice among religious, ethnic, or cultural education streams that are publicly funded while enjoying some degree of administrative and pedagogical autonomy; such systems can be found in the Netherlands, Israel, and other countries. In the present chapter we consider an education system modeled on local education in the United States, in which parents can individually choose to opt out of public education and instead send their children to private schools. However, opting out of public education does not reduce their liability to pay the education tax that funds public schools, effectively requiring them to pay twice for their children's education. This creates a strong incentive for parents to remain within the public system and effectively limits school choice, especially for the less affluent. Supporters of the system see two central advantages in its uniformity: it promises equal opportunity for all and creates a shared education experience that acts as a cohesive element in a diverse society that continues to absorb large numbers of immigrants.

Recent years have seen growing support for increased variety in publicly financed education—whether through vouchers or tax credits or through greater autonomy for individual schools. Some argue for greater school choice on egalitarian grounds, noting that the local organization of education in the United States links education quality to residential location and thus conditions educational opportunities within the *public* school system on parents' material resources. School choice offers disadvantaged children trapped in failing public school systems a way out. Some argue on libertarian grounds, maintaining that parents have a basic right to shape their children's education, a right that should not be limited only to those who can afford to pay private-school tuition or reside in a school district that offers the type of education they desire. And many advocate school choice for efficiency reasons, whether because they deem private schools to be more efficient than public schools or because the option to choose private education exerts competitive pressure on public schools to operate more efficiently.[1] By devolving authority to individual schools, school choice weakens the influence of inflated central bureaucracies, reduces overheads, and reinforces parents' active involvement in their children's education (Metz, 1990). Furthermore, school autonomy allows wider experimentation with new methods of teaching and organization, which benefits all schools (Hassel, 1998).

Skeptics question whether school choice will indeed serve the interests of the disadvantaged, pointing out that parents with lower incomes and less education are less likely to make the best use of school choice, possibly leaving the neediest children with the worst choices.[2] This is further aggravated if elitist private schools are allowed to apply discriminatory admissions criteria—while benefiting from public support—that will increase racial and socioeconomic segregation in schools. Moreover, busing promising pupils out of their inner-city minority communities drains the brightest pupils from these communities and further weakens them.[3] Concerns such as these have led supporters of school choice to incorporate these criticisms in shaping school-choice programs that better meet the needs of disadvantaged children. Current voucher programs typically restrict eligibility to low-income families, actively disseminate information to eligible parents and provide counseling to those who seek it, require participating schools to accept all applicants (or choose among them randomly), and so on. Opponents of school choice maintain that public funds would be better spent on improving public schools in failing districts rather than offering students a way out.[4]

The contemporary history of school choice in the United States can be traced to Friedman's (1962) advocacy of a universal voucher system, modeled on the success of the GI Bill, which financed the further education of World War II veterans in the institutions of their choice, public or private. However, early experiments with elementary and high school vouchers failed to mobilize significant public support. Many taxpayers viewed voucher programs as inappropriately using their tax dollars to subsidize the private education of the wealthy and undermine the values that public education represents; teachers' unions opposed the weakening of public education, through vouchers, for professional reasons.

Only more recently has increasing dissatisfaction with the quality of public schooling in disadvantaged areas renewed the momentum for school choice.[5] Experimentation with publicly funded vouchers was revived in 1990, when Wisconsin's Milwaukee Parental Choice Program introduced a small-scale program limited to nonsectarian schools. When in 1995 it sought also to include religious schools, constitutional challenges delayed the change until the Wisconsin Supreme Court gave its approval in 1998. Ohio's Cleveland Scholarship Program, implemented in 1996, was the first publicly funded program to allow vouchers to be applied toward tuition in religious schools, its constitutionality affirmed by the U.S. Supreme Court in 2002 in its landmark decision on *Zelman v. Simmons-Harris*.[6] A third program, in Florida, offering vouchers to children in failing school districts was approved in 1999. There are no other publicly funded voucher programs currently operating in the United States.[7]

Other initiatives, aimed at providing greater choice *within* the public school system, are gaining wider currency. The largely local control of education in the United States produces in itself a variety of schooling options, but these are tied to residential location, and so the choices that the public school system offers are very much constrained by income. Choice within the public system is achieved by severing the link between residential location and schooling options. In large school districts this can be achieved through open registration that asks incoming pupils to list their schooling preferences and allocates them to the schools of their choice, to the extent possible. The federal No Child Left Behind Act requires that students in failing schools be allowed to move to better schools. Charter schools—publicly financed, autonomous, often specialized schools that accept pupils from extensive catchment areas—offer specific choices within the public school system (Finn et al., 2000).[8] Introducing effective choice within the public system is a way of mimicking the action of market forces traditionally absent from public education.

The education systems of New Zealand and Chile (described in chapter 2) have gone furthest in offering parents a choice of schooling options. New Zealand began implementing a "universal quasi-voucher system" in 1989, devolving control of education from a central Ministry of Education to the management boards of individual schools. Each school receives government funding based on student enrollment and enjoys extensive freedom to pursue its goals within broad guidelines, with the government functioning primarily in an oversight capacity (Fiske and Ladd, 2000). The large majority of students continue to attend state-owned schools, but these schools now enjoy a large measure of individual autonomy, effectively operating as an ideal type of charter school. Chile's universal school voucher program, implemented in the early 1980s, relies more heavily on private schools. Students who wish to exit the public system can choose between established Catholic schools and newly created private-sector secular schools (Hsieh and Urquiola, 2003). In both countries, the new systems appear to have caused increased sorting by ability and income. This allows able and motivated children from disadvantaged backgrounds to escape the poorer schools that hold them back but also aggravates the problems of these weaker schools. In some cases the central government has resumed direct control of the weakest of these schools.[9]

In the following sections we first examine a basic model of "opting out" of public education and then extend it to allow for variety in religious preferences. This is followed by an elementary analysis of the interaction among local public education, residential migration, and private schools. We conclude the chapter with an analysis of the effect of education vouchers on enrollment and education spending.

A Basic Model of "Opting Out" of Public Education

We begin with a basic model of opting out of a public school system funded by an education tax that must be paid regardless of whether or not the taxpayer's child studies in a public school. It shares many of the premises of the education models considered in the previous chapters, with the important exception that private education is available as an exclusive *alternative* to public schooling.[10] Initially, we allow households to vary only in their incomes; this variation drives demand for private education.

Consider an economy with a fixed, heterogeneous population of households indexed by i. Let y_i denote household income, and let $F(y)$ denote its cumulative distribution function. As in the preceding chapters, households derive utility from consumption c and from the quality of their children's education s, which they identify with spending per student;[11] and all are assumed to have the same constant elasticity of substitution (CES) utility function

$$U(c,s) = c^{(1-1/\sigma)}/(1 - 1/\sigma) + \delta s^{(1-1/\sigma)}/(1 - 1/\sigma). \tag{7.1}$$

Public education is available free of charge to all households at a uniform quality funded by a proportional income tax rate τ levied on all households and determined by majority vote. Parents wishing to opt out of public education can instead purchase private education, in any desired quality, from a competitive private-school sector.[12] However, this does not reduce their tax liability.

Let q denote the proportion of households that use the public school system. The government's balanced-budget constraint implies that spending per pupil in public schooling, which equals $\tau Y/q$, is inversely related to the proportion of children in public education. Then household i expects that if it sends its child to public school, its utility is given by the indirect utility function $V(\tau, q^e, y_i)$, where q^e denotes the level of public enrollment it anticipates when making its education decision.[13] It follows from the shape of the utility function that V is initially increasing in τ and then decreasing: at low levels of spending, raising the tax rate increases household utility; at high levels, further increases reduces utility (see figure 7.1).

A household that considers sending its child to private school maximizes its utility subject to the budget constraint $c + s = (1 - \tau)y_i$. We denote the indirect utility derived from private schooling by $W(\tau, y_i)$ and allow for the possibility that parents perceive a dollar spent on private education as more (or less) effective than a dollar spent on public education.[14] The utility of a household that opts out of public education is not affected by the improved quality of public education, and hence its indirect utility varies inversely with the tax rate τ.[15] Once the tax rate has been determined by voting, each household i chooses between public and private education by comparing $V(\tau, q^e, y_i)$ to $W(\tau, y_i)$. In figure 7.1, if the tax rate is set at $\underline{\tau}$, household i will choose to send its child to a public school, as $V(\underline{\tau}, q^e, y_i) > W(\underline{\tau}, y_i)$.

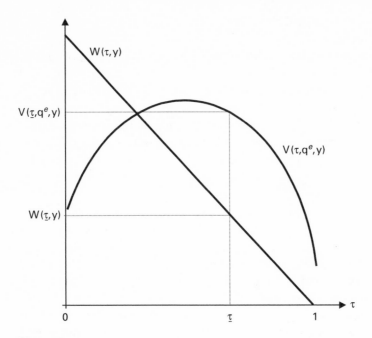

Figure 7.1
Choosing between public and private education

Assume all households anticipate the same public enrollment q^e. Then for a given tax level τ, either all households prefer public education, or there exists a threshold income level $y = y(\tau, q^e)$, implicitly defined by equating the utility attained from attending a public school to the utility of opting out—setting $V(\tau, q^e, y) = W(\tau, y)$—such that all households with income below y send their children to public school and all those with income above y sends their children to private school. Private education makes sense only if the better education it offers outweighs the loss of consumption entailed; as households are identical except in income, this applies only to higher-income households with lower marginal utility from consumption.[16] We require that in equilibrium anticipated public-school enrollment q^e equals actual enrollment given the tax rate τ—that is, that $q^e = F(y(\tau, q^e))$.

Now consider the political determination of the education tax rate by a majority vote of households, with each household voting to maximize its anticipated utility. As householders can choose between public and private education after the tax level has been set, they consider the effect of the tax rate on the envelope of the indirect utility functions,

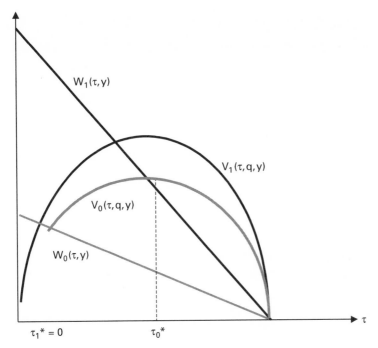

Figure 7.2
Voting on the tax level

W and V. Figure 7.2 depicts the envelope functions of two households: subscript 1 designates the richer household of the two, and 0 designates the poorer household.

The richer household in figure 7.2 prefers a zero tax level, as it derives greater utility from private schooling than from any level of public schooling. The poorer household anticipates that it will use public education and prefers the positive tax rate τ_0^* at which V attains its maximal value. This is the tax rate that optimally balances spending on consumption with spending on education, taking into account the household's implicit tax-price of education—determined by the ratio of household income to average income and by the public enrollment share q.

Taking the partial derivative of $\partial V/\partial \tau$ with respect to y, when the elasticity of substitution σ is greater than one, the preferred tax rate decreases with income among households that prefer public to private schooling. As higher-income households that anticipate opting out of public education prefer a zero tax rate, this implies that the preferred tax rate decreases monotonically throughout the entire range of incomes; that, from the single crossing property, a political equilibrium exists; and that the chosen tax rate is the tax rate preferred by the median-income household.[17] The income of the decisive voter y_d, satisfies in this case

$$F(y_d) = \tfrac{1}{2}. \tag{7.2a}$$

Conversely, when the elasticity of substitution σ is less than one, the preferred tax rate increases with income among households that prefer public schooling. This implies that an "ends against the middle" coalition is formed: the poor, who prefer less public spending on education, join forces with the rich, who would rather send their children to private schools and therefore prefer a zero tax rate, in opposition to the middle class, who want higher spending levels.[18] In this case, the single-crossing property does not generally hold, and a global political equilibrium may not exist. Epple and Romano (1996a) show that a political equilibrium of this type must satisfy the necessary condition[19]

$$F(y_d) = q - 0.5, \tag{7.2b}$$

where again y_d denotes the income of the decisive household; as $q \leq 1$, it is no greater than median income.

Religious Preferences

The basic model described above has been used to model school choice in various contexts, but it omits several important dimensions. In this section we consider the unique role of religious education; in the next, we consider residential location.

Religious education merits explicit recognition in an analysis of school choice because of its numbers—in the United States approximately five out of every six private-school students attend religious schools—and its special attributes.[20] Tuition in religious schools is often subsidized from church funds, private donations, and the willingness of teachers in religious orders to accept reduced salaries, rendering it generally more accessible than nonsectarian private schools to low-income households.[21] At the same time, parents' attitudes to these schools are strongly influenced by nonmonetary factors. These two facets of religious education explain why parents are willing to "pay twice" to send their children to religious schools, though spending per pupil in these schools is often considerably lower than in public schools;[22] and they accord with the observed heterogeneity of incomes among households that choose private schools. In addition, in the United States, religious education merits explicit modeling because of the constitutional separation of church and state, which limits the use of publicly financed vouchers to support religious education.[23]

To explicitly address these issues, we introduce in our model a third type of school, private religious schools, and assign to each household an individual utility parameter z_i that reflects its innate preference for religious schooling:[24] households with $z_i < 1$ view religious schooling as a drawback, though they may opt for a religious school if it is sufficiently subsidized (and their value of z_i is not too small), while households with $z_i > 1$ view religious schooling as an advantage. Household utility then depends on consumption, on spending per pupil in the child's school, and on the religious orientation of the household's school of choice given its preference for religious schooling. Extending the utility function in (7.1), the utility of a household with religious preference z_i equals

$$U(c_i, s_i, z_i) = \begin{cases} c_i^{(1-1/\sigma)}/(1 - 1/\sigma) + \delta(z_i s_i)^{(1-1/\sigma)}/(1 - 1/\sigma) \\ \quad \text{in a religious school,} \\ c_i^{(1-1/\sigma)}/(1 - 1/\sigma) + \delta s_i^{(1-1/\sigma)}/(1 - 1/\sigma) \\ \quad \text{in a secular school.} \end{cases} \qquad (7.3)$$

Households now have three schooling options from which to choose: public secular, private secular, and private religious. As before, public education is available free of charge to all households in uniform quality, and both religious and nonsectarian private schooling can be purchased from a competitively priced private sector in any desired quality, as alternatives to public schooling, albeit without reducing one's tax liability. We assume that while the cost of a unit of education quality in nonsectarian private schools is the same as in public schools, its cost in religious schools may be privately subsidized at the uniform rate $r \leq 1$, and denote $k_i = z_i/(1 - r)$.

Again, as opting out of public education does not reduce one's tax obligations, sending one's child to private school must be aimed at obtaining a better education. However, it is no longer the case that income solely determines school choice: low-income parents with sufficiently high values of k_i, reflecting the combined effect of subsidies and religious sentiment, choose religious schooling. Figure 7.3 illustrates the division of the population among the three types of schools, highlighting the heterogeneity of incomes among households that

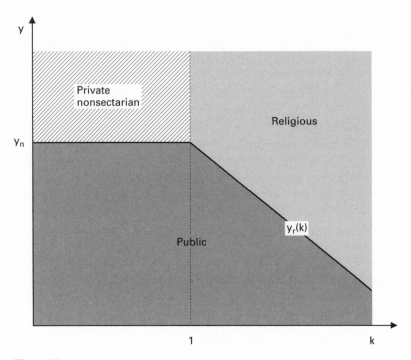

Figure 7.3
The distribution of religious and secular households among school types (schematic representation)

send their children to religious private schools. Cohen-Zada and Just-man (2002) fully characterize a political-economic equilibrium with religious private schools and calibrate the parameters of the model to observed enrollment shares and tax rates. Their findings indicate strong tacit demand for religious education in the United States, which is not realized because of the need to pay twice for religious schooling. If parents were not required to pay twice for religious education and current, subsidized tuition levels could be maintained, religious enrollment would increase dramatically. However, this depends critically on tuition subsidies keeping pace with expanded enrollment. Absent subsidies, the level of demand for religious education would decline sharply.

Residential Mobility and School Choice

The large proportion of local revenues in education funding in the United States—over 40 percent in 1999–2000—reflects the dependence of school choice on residential location. Models of school choice that incorporate location decisions are closely related to the more general literature on local public goods and residential mobility. Recent extensions of these models incorporate multiple dimensions of variation in household attributes and specific institutional detail.[25] Here we present a simplified model that illustrates how individual decisions on school choice and democratic decisions on school funding can be integrated in a model of location with peer-group effects and a competitive housing market. It demonstrates that encouraging households to opt out of public education can reduce residential segregation (Nechyba, 2000, 2003).

Consider an economy with two school districts, indexed by $j = a, b$, with fixed housing supply H_j in district j; and two types of household, poor and rich, indexed by $i = p, r$. There are n_p poor households with income y_p and n_r rich households with income y_r, where $y_p < y_r$. To simplify the analysis we assume that income is exogenous and housing is rented from external landlords. The housing market in each district is competitive, and we denote by p_j the price of housing in district j. Households are identical in all aspects other than income, and each has one school-age child. Each household derives utility from a numeraire consumption good c, education quality e, and housing h; and all have the same logarithmic utility function

$$U(c, e, h) = \alpha \ln c + \beta \ln e + (1 - \alpha - \beta) \ln h. \tag{7.4}$$

Education quality e is a product of school spending per pupil s and peer-group quality θ, which we identify with average household income in the school and to fix ideas posit $e = s\theta^{\gamma/\beta}$. Spending per student in public schools is determined in each district by a vote on the district tax rate t_j, determining total school spending in the district, which is then divided by public enrollment in the district. Spending per student in private schools is determined individually. Peer quality in public education equals average district income. Peer quality in private education equals individual income (as we have assumed away scale effects, and no one would wish to have their child study with someone from a lower-income household).

Householders must decide, in sequence, in which district to reside, how to vote on the tax rate, whether to send their children to public or private school, and how to divide their disposable income between consumption, housing, and, if chosen, private schooling. An equilibrium comprises

• A division of households between districts and types of school,

• School tax rates t_a and t_b, and

• Housing prices p_a and p_b,

such that

• No household wishes to move from its district or change its school type,

• Each tax rate commands a majority in its district over any alternative rate,

• Each household is maximizing its utility given prices and tax rates, and

• Housing markets clear in each district.

Assume initially, as a benchmark, that private schooling is not available and that a segregating equilibrium holds, as in the Tiebout model in chapter 6, such that all rich households reside in district a and all poor households reside in district b. As both districts are homogeneous, voting is trivial. Spending on consumption, public schooling, and housing is proportional to the coefficients of the utility function, and housing prices are derived from the market-clearing condition.[26] For this to be an equilibrium it must be the case that neither type of household wishes to move, which holds if and only if the higher housing price in district a exactly balances the advantage of its better schools. A comparison of utilities reveals that this holds when

$$(\beta + \gamma) \ln(y_r/y_p) = (1 - \alpha - \beta) \ln(p_a/p_b). \tag{7.5}$$

Assume that this condition holds, so that absent private education a segregating equilibrium would obtain, and consider the effect of allowing individual households to opt out of public education and choose private schooling instead while continuing to pay the education tax. Comparing the utility of a rich household before and after moving to the poor district, we find that if the difference in housing prices is large enough (which holds if the difference in incomes between rich and poor is large enough), then it is worthwhile for the rich household to move to the poorer district and take advantage of its lower housing price while opting out of its inferior school system.[27] Thus for some parameter values, allowing households to opt out of public education and choose private education at their own expense reduces residential segregation. If this happens, housing prices in the poor district with inferior public schooling will rise, while those in the rich district with better public schooling will fall. Whether less residential segregation is a Pareto improvement that increases the utility of all households depends on whether the poor households in district *b* gain more from the added tax income they receive from the rich migrant household than they lose from a higher housing price. The rich households remaining in district *a* are certainly better off, as they have improved their housing (there are fewer of them to divide a fixed supply) while losing nothing in education quality or consumption.

Vouchers or tax credits that partly offset the cost of private education lower the rich household's cost of moving to the poor district and opting for private schooling. Thus vouchers or tax credits increase the range of parameter values for which private education reduces residential segregation, raise housing prices in the district with inferior public schooling, and lower them in the district with better public schooling.

The Effect of School Vouchers on Enrollment and Spending

There is very little practical experience with vouchers in the United States from which their effects on enrollment and spending can be gauged, and so such effects are frequently estimated by simulating calibrated models of school choice.[28] Many such studies have been carried out in stylized settings that are similar to the calibrated models described in preceding sections, and several recent studies—Nechyba (2000) is a prominent example—have enriched the basic model with added structure and institutional detail. While specific results invariably depend on the details of the application, several general conclusions can nevertheless be drawn from these studies.

A voucher program has a beneficial fiscal effect—it raises public spending per pupil holding the school tax rate fixed—if savings to the public purse as a result of exits from the public school system, which the voucher program induces, are greater than the cost of the voucher program. This will depend very much on the scope and design of the system, as Levin and Driver (1997) point out, and can hold only if the sum of the voucher is less than average cost savings per exiting pupil.[29] Thus savings increase directly with the reduction in public enrollment and fall with the number of voucher recipients who would have attended private schools even without vouchers. Limiting voucher eligibility to low-income families not able to afford private schooling without a voucher increases the likelihood of a beneficial fiscal effect.

Retaining the notation of preceding sections, we can compute a necessary condition for the reduction in public enrollment to generate an increase in public spending per pupil. Assuming that savings from reduced public enrollment equals average spending per pupil—a long-term view—we find that if spending per pupil is to increase, holding tax revenues constant, public enrollment after the voucher is implemented must be less than the threshold value q^* given by

$$\tau Y / q_0 = [\tau Y - (1 - q^*)xm]/q^*, \tag{7.6}$$

where q_0 is public enrollment before the voucher program is implemented, x is the size of the voucher, and m is the number of school-age children per household.[30]

Incorporating religious preferences in simulating the effect of voucher programs highlights the practical importance of the religious dimension of private education (Cohen-Zada and Justman, 2002). Restricting vouchers to nonsectarian schools virtually precludes their use by lower-income households unless they are offered in very generous amounts. Low-income families will use a voucher only if it is sufficient in itself to obtain a better education than local public schools can offer. If voucher amounts are not large, only subsidized religious schools will accept them in full payment of tuition.[31] Nonsectarian schools that do not have access to similar charitable sources will require additional tuition.[32] The public voucher programs in Milwaukee and Cleveland, which include religious schools, illustrate this point well. In Cleveland, where smaller vouchers of up to $2,250 were offered to low-income parents of children in grades K–7, 96 percent of participating children enrolled in religious schools. In Milwaukee, which offered vouchers exceeding $5,000 to low-income families, one third of recipients chose nonsectarian schools, almost all of these in elementary schools. These findings support the conclusion implicit in the Supreme Court's ruling in *Zelman v. Simmons-Harris* that the primary objective of Ohio's pilot voucher program—to provide greater educational opportunity for underprivileged students in a failing public school system—could not have been achieved at similar cost if the program had excluded religious schools.

However, lessons learned from small-scale voucher experiments may not be applicable to large-scale programs. Calibrations indicate that demand for religious education is strongly dependent on current subsidy levels (Cohen-Zada and Justman, 2002), which may not be sustainable if enrollment markedly increases. Moreover, political support for large-scale programs will depend not only on the preferences of parents with school-age children but also on how such programs are expected to affect property values (Brunner and Sonstelie, 2003). As the preceding analysis indicates, unrestricted vouchers allow high-income households to take advantage of low housing prices in neighborhoods with inferior public schools while opting out of these public schools without paying the full cost of private education (Nechyba, 2000). This raises real estate values in school districts with inferior public schooling while lowering values in districts with superior public schools. Brunner and Sonstelie (2003) show that these considerations influenced voting on a voucher initiative proposed in California in 2000. In addition, while small-scale programs designed to help the neediest of children may be tolerated on compassionate grounds, large-scale voucher programs are widely viewed by education professionals with a stake in the public school system as posing an unacceptable threat to the system. Finally, large-scale voucher programs can have a substantial effect on the cultural fabric of society, an issue we consider further in chapter 8.

Conclusions

In this chapter we considered the interaction between public and private education in the context of an education system modeled on local education in the United States, in which parents may individually choose to opt out of public education, may instead send their children to private schools, but must continue to pay the education tax that funds public schools. This creates a strong incentive for all but the very affluent or religiously committed to keep their children in public education.

A simple model of opting out served as the basis of our analysis, demonstrating the different political equilibria that may arise: a "median-income" equilibrium in which poor are aligned against rich and an "ends-against-the-middle" equilibrium in which the poor and the rich join forces against the middle class. Which equilibrium holds depends on the parameter values of the utility function.

We then extended the model to include religious education, reflecting the predominantly religious nature of private schooling in the United States, the special status of religious schools, and the heterogeneity in incomes of households that choose private education. Calibrations indicate strong tacit demand for religious education in the United States, which is not realized because of the need to pay twice for religious schooling. However, this depends critically on tuition subsidies keeping pace with expanded enrollment; absent subsidies, the level of demand for religious education would decline sharply. These findings point to the need for further work on the supply of religious schooling.

A further extension, incorporating school choice in a model of residential location, showed how school choice and education vouchers can reduce income-based residential segregation while raising housing prices in districts with inferior public schools and reducing them in districts with better public school systems. Further work is needed to integrate religious preferences, residential location, and the supply of private schooling in the political economy of public education.

We then considered some fiscal aspects of voucher programs, describing general conditions that must hold for a voucher to increase public spending per pupil and highlighting the importance of the religious dimension for voucher programs in the United States. Initiatives to provide modest vouchers to low-income families in failing school districts, to be used in either secular or religious schools, proved to be both constitutionally acceptable and politically feasible in Cleveland and Milwaukee. However, extending such programs to broader constituencies will stretch the supply of affordable religious education and may not pass constitutional review. Moreover, its political fortune will depend not only on its affect on households with school-age children but also on its anticipated affect on real estate prices and on the communal values that the public-school movement embodies. The link between public schooling and communal values is the subject of our next chapter.

8   Education, Social Capital, and the Dynamics of Cohesion

The Lord came down to look at the city and tower that man had built, and the Lord said, "If, as one people with one language for all, this is how they have begun to act, then nothing that they may propose to do will be out of their reach. Let us, then, go down and confound their speech there, so that they shall not understand one another's speech."

—Genesis, 11:5–7

Economic analysis, in emphasizing the contribution of education to growth and development, has focused on the instrumental role of education in building human capital by teaching productive skills. This has obscured its socializing role in building social norms and a common culture, the importance of which has long been widely recognized by students and practitioners of education alike.[1] As we observed in chapter 2, the emergence of government involvement in education in the eighteenth and nineteenth centuries was closely tied to this socializing role, as a means of establishing the legitimacy of new secular regimes and promoting the cohesion of newly formed national entities (Good and Teller, 1969; Green, 1990).[2]

In this chapter we focus on this latter role of public education: its contribution to social cohesion, an aspect emphasized by Emile Durkheim (1956/1922, p. 70), a pioneer of the sociology of education:

Society can only exist if there exists among its members a sufficient degree of homogeneity. Education perpetuates and reinforces this homogeneity by fixing in the child, from the beginning, the essential similarities that collective life demands.

This contribution is of greatest importance in two primary settings. It has a central role to play in the formation of new unified national identity from diverse local cultures and allegiances; this was its role in nineteenth-century France and Germany and more recently in the many multiethnic nations that emerged in Africa and Asia in the second half of the twentieth century. And it plays a key role in immigrant societies, such as the United States, where centralized public schooling has contributed significantly to the cultural and economic assimilation of immigrants (Edwards and Richey, 1963; Bowles and Gintis, 1976).

Recognizing this socializing role of education goes a long way toward explaining the ubiquitous role of the public sector in the provision and not only financing of primary and high school education. As we emphasized in chapter 1, education is both appropriable and divisible and so does not have the technical attributes of a public good. The reasons frequently given for the large role of the public sector in education—external benefits, capital-market imperfections, an innate preference for equal opportunity—could be addressed largely without direct administrative intervention in the schooling process, such as through the use of subsidies or vouchers. It is the socializing role of education that presents a need for more direct intervention, inasmuch as cultural content is difficult to monitor at arm's length without the direct controls of public administration (Lott, 1990; Usher, 1977; Kremer and Sarychev, 1998).

An emerging body of empirical studies attests to the effect of social cohesion on economic performance. These studies, drawing on conceptual foundations laid down by Coleman (1988), Fukuyama (1995), and Putnam (1993), develop explicit operational measures of social ties, trust, voluntarism, and social participation and relate them to economic growth and other measures of performance. One strand of this literature uses cross-country regressions to identify a positive effect on growth of various manifestations of social capital such as participation in voluntary associations, the degree of trust, and corruption (e.g., Knack and Keefer, 1997; Temple and Johnson, 1998; La Porta et al., 1997; Zak and Knack, 2001). Other studies, such as Greif (1993) and Kotkin (1992), document the high intensity of economic activity within ethnic groups and its economic benefits for group members in specific cases. Yet another set of empirical studies addresses the economic consequences of residential segregation in ethnic enclaves: Lazear (1999) presents evidence on the effect of such segregation on fluency in English among immigrants to the United States, and Edin et al. (2003) use a natural experiment afforded by a policy shift in immigrant settlement in Sweden to show that immigrants, especially those who are less skilled, derive a substantial return from living within the boundaries of such an enclave.

This is the theme of the following analysis: social norms and cultural values shape economic outcomes, and so the success of an education system in instilling these norms and values affects economic performance, apart from its role in the accumulation of human capital.[3]

Education and the Dynamics of Social Polarization

A simple illustration of the effects of education on social cohesion can be given by studying an extension of the model of chapter 5, where the production function is augmented by an additional input related to social cohesion. Following Gradstein and Justman (2002) we assume that individual income is, at least from some point on, a decreasing function of average social distance from one's cohort, which results from the social orientation of one's schooling. Parents concerned for their children's material well-being can contribute to it by raising them in the mainstream common culture, but only at the emotional cost of diluting the traditional values in which the parents themselves were raised and thus weakening the bond between parent and child. This implies that parents' decisions on the social orientation of their own children have external effects on the productivity of other children, indicating that without centralized intervention social polarization will be excessively large. A concerted homogenization of the social content of education can therefore reduce transaction costs in the next generation and thereby enhance economic efficiency.

To focus on cultural differences among households, we assume that initially all parents are exogenously endowed with the same income y_0 but differ in their social orientations, which we represent in the abstract by a single parameter $0 \leq p \leq 1$, where p_{it} denotes the social orientation of parent i in period t. We assume for simplicity that generation 0 comprises two uniform social groups of equal size, "reds" and "greens" (denoted r and g), with initial social characteristics $p_{r0} < p_{g0}$ located symmetrically in the unit interval, $p_{r0} = 1 - p_{g0}$; and denote the initial degree of social polarization $\Delta_0 = p_{g0} - p_{r0}$. The social distance between parent and child determines the degree of alienation between them, $C(|p_{it} - p_{it+1}|)$, which directly reduces parental utility, albeit at a diminishing rate, $C' > 0$, $C'' < 0$; we set $C(0) = 0$.

The social distance between an individual and other members of her cohort affects the productivity of her instrumental human capital. While some degree of cultural heterogeneity clearly offers economic benefits, empirical evidence from a variety of sources illustrates the harm that can come from deep cultural divides. Mauro's (1995) cross-country analysis finds that social polarization adversely affects the quality of services provided by the central government and generates political instability. Easterly and Levine's (1997) analysis of a cross-section of countries similarly finds that it promotes corruption and rent-seeking and causes inefficient policies resulting in poor infrastructure, a lack of financial institutions and low educational achievement—leading them to conclude that ethnic heterogeneity is the main source of backwardness in Africa. DiPasquale and Glaeser (1998), using both U.S. and international data, show that ethnic diversity is a significant determinant of urban unrest. Several studies examine the effect of ethnic and racial heterogeneity on the provision of publicly provided goods in a cross-section of local communities in the United States and find it has a negative impact (Alesina et al., 1999; Alesina and La Ferrara, 2000; Goldin and Katz, 1999; Poterba, 1997), and there is evidence that this holds true elsewhere as well, such as Miguel and Gugerty's (2002) similar findings for rural communities in Kenya. More directly, Glaeser et al. (1995) find that racial heterogeneity negatively affects municipal growth in the United States.

To make explicit the effect of social distance on income we define a metric $D(|p_{it+1} - p_{jt+1}|) \geq 0$ that represents the expected productivity of a transaction between two members of the same cohort i and j. It can be thought of as a function of two opposing forces: the probability that, given the opportunity to cooperate, i and j will effect a successful transaction between them, which we assume to be a decreasing function of the cultural distance that separates them; and the advantages of cooperation when a transaction has been successfully concluded, which may increase with cultural diversity. We set $D(0) = 1$ and assume that it is twice differentiable and concave, allowing that D may increase with cultural distance at low levels of polarization but requiring that it decreases from some point on—that is, requiring that there exists a threshold level $\underline{\Delta} \geq 0$ such that D is decreasing when $|p_i - p_j|$ exceeds $\underline{\Delta}$, so that $\underline{\Delta}$ is a global maximum of D.[4] We assume that the initial level of polarization Δ_0 exceeds this threshold, $\Delta_0 \geq \underline{\Delta}$.

Exchange and production in the economy result from the random matching of pairs of individuals to perform transactions.[5] A match between individuals i and j with human-capital levels h_{it} and h_{jt} and social orientations p_{it} and p_{jt} produces income $Ah_{it}D(|p_{it} - p_{jt}|)$ for individual i and $Ah_{jt}D(|p_{it} - p_{jt}|)$ for individual j, where A is a positive constant. Letting F_t denote the cumulative distribution function of cultural orientation in period t, individual i's expected value of D in random encounters with other members of its cohort is

$$\Pi_t(p_{it}) = \int D(|p_{it} - p_{kt}|)\, dF_t(k). \tag{8.1}$$

Individual i's expected income in period t is then proportional to the product of this expected value and her instrumental human capital,

$$y_{it} = Ah_{it}\Pi(p_{it}). \tag{8.2}$$

The utility that the parent of household i in period t seeks to maximize is then an increasing function of current household consumption and of her child's expected income and a decreasing function of the social distance between parent and child. To fix ideas, we set

$$U(c_{it}, p_{it}, y_{it+1}) = \log(c_{it}) - C(|p_{it} - p_{it+1}|) + \delta \log(y_{it+1}). \tag{8.3}$$

This is maximized by dividing current income y_{it} between consumption c_{it} and instrumental investment in the child's human capital h_{it+1}, subject to the budget constraint $y_{it} = c_{it} + h_{it+1}$; and by choosing the social orientation of the child's schooling p_{it+1}, which for simplicity we assume entirely determines the child's social orientation.[6] We compare how this is done under different schooling regimes.

Consider initially a *decentralized sectoral schooling* regime in which there exist separate schools for the members of the two groups, so that education decisions are made communally within each group and education is uniform within each group. As we have assumed that social orientation is exclusively determined at school and both groups are initially uniform, this implies that they will remain so in subsequent periods, and we denote by p_{rt} and p_{gt} their respective social orientations in period t.

The parents of each group then choose h_{jt+1} and p_{jt+1} in each period to maximize their respective utilities. Maximization of (8.3) with respect to the amount of instrumental investment in human capital h_{jt+1} subject to equations (8.1) and (8.2) and the budget constraint yields the optimal value of $h_{jt+1} = [\delta/(1 + \delta)]y_{jt}$. Maximization with respect to social orientation is more complex. Note that it can never be optimal for parents to choose for their children a social orientation more extreme than their own as this would be twice harmful, increasing the generation gap between parent and child and decreasing the child's future

income. By similar reasoning, households never reduce the level of social polarization below $\underline{\Delta}$, the level at which productivity is maximal.
The degree of social polarization in period t, $\Delta_t = |p_{gt} - p_{rt}|$, is there-
fore nonincreasing over time.[7] The first-order condition yields the
following characterization of the evolution of social orientation along
interior points on the equilibrium transition path:[8]

$$C'(\tfrac{1}{2}(\Delta_t - \Delta_{t+1})) + \delta D'(\Delta_{t+1})/[1 + D(\Delta_{t+1})] = 0, \quad (\Delta_t > \Delta_{t+1}). \tag{8.4}$$

Next-period income is then identical across individuals and equals

$$y_{t+1} = \tfrac{1}{2}A[\delta/(1+\delta)][1 + D(\Delta_{t+1})]y_t. \tag{8.5}$$

This implies that the growth rate, $\lambda_t = y_{t+1}/y_t = \tfrac{1}{2}A[\delta/(1+\delta)] \cdot [1 + D(\Delta_{t+1})]$, is declining in the degree of social polarization. Hence,
along the equilibrium transition path, before the economy is in a
steady state, social polarization is decreasing and the growth rate is
increasing, suggesting that education and wage differentials between
different ethnic groups should diminish from one generation to another. Defining the economy to be in steady state when the degree
of social polarization is stationary, $\Delta_t = \Delta_{t+1}$, the monotonicity of Δ_t
along the equilibrium path implies that the economy must converge to
a steady state of social polarization Δ, illustrated in figure 8.1. It can
be shown to be unique and thus independent of the initial conditions.
Equation (8.5) implies that the steady-state rate of growth is inversely
related to social polarization.

Welfare Implications of Different Schooling Regimes

We next examine the welfare implications of decentralized schooling
and compare it to centralized schooling. As a benchmark, consider the
Pareto-optimal trajectory of social orientation of schooling p_{it+1} and investment in instrumental human capital h_{it+1}, subject to a balanced-
budget constraint in each period. Because of the inherent symmetry
between the two groups and the uniformity of households within
groups, we limit our attention to Pareto-optimal allocations that
are uniform within social groups and symmetric around $p = \tfrac{1}{2}$. All
individuals then have the same amount of instrumental human capital in each period, and income evolves according to the following
equation:[9]

$$y_{t+1} = Ah_{t+1}[1 + D(\Delta_{t+1})]/2. \tag{8.6}$$

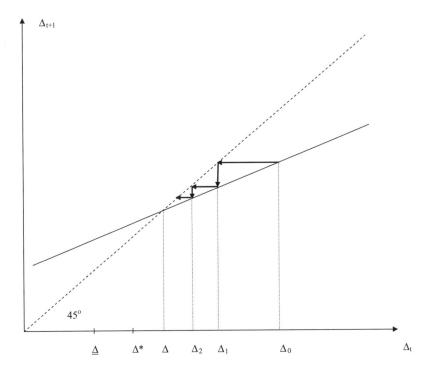

Figure 8.1
Convergence to the decentralized steady-state level of polarization

This absence of intertemporal dependence implies that efficient allocations can be characterized by independent maximization of utility in each period,

$$U_t = \log(c_t) - C(\tfrac{1}{2}(\Delta_t - \Delta_{t+1})) + \delta \log(y_{t+1}). \tag{8.7}$$

Solving this, we obtain that a necessary condition for socially optimal accumulation of human capital is $h_{t+1} = [\delta/(1 + \delta)]y_t$, so that the same share of income is allocated to schooling as under decentralization. The optimal intertemporal evolution of social orientation at interior points is given by

$$\tfrac{1}{2}C'(\tfrac{1}{2}(\Delta_t - \Delta_{t+1})) + \delta D'(\Delta_{t+1})/[1 + D(\Delta_{t+1})] = 0, \tag{8.8}$$

which implies that Δ_t cannot increase along the optimal path, and as Δ_t is bounded, it must converge to a steady-state Δ^*, which must be unique from the concavity of D.

Comparing the socially optimal solution to the equilibrium transition path under sectoral schooling, we observe that polarization is reduced more slowly under sectoral schooling. Thus under sectoral schooling, polarization is excessive, and growth is slower in each period and in the steady state, compared to the optimal path (see figure 8.1). The reason for this inefficiency of decentralized schooling is that each community, when making its educational decisions, disregards the benefits to the rival community of reduced polarization.

A regime of coordinated decentralized schooling in which the two communities maintain separate curricula that are centrally regulated to avoid excessive polarization achieves a faster rate of growth. This indicates a potentially important normative role for government education policy in coordinating a reciprocal homogenization of sectoral school systems. However, this may be difficult to achieve. One type of difficulty arises because agreements between sectors regarding the dynamic evolution of curriculum content must be difficult to formulate and monitor.[10] Another type of difficulty that arises in a polarized context in which all agents are identified with one group or another is the absence of an impartial enforcement agency. When this is the case, the cultural orientation of the education system is shaped by political action reflecting the balance of political power as it is mediated by institutional factors.[11] This leads us to ask how the parameters of the political process might affect the social orientation of a centralized education system compared to decentralized schooling. Clearly, much depends on the details of the political process, which can be modeled in more than one way.

Consider, for example, a political regime of representative democracy with legislative bargaining—this follows a reduced-form model of legislative bargaining introduced by Besley and Coate (1998)—and assume there is a government that determines the size of the education budget and the social orientation of the two sectoral school systems in each period. Then if all tax revenues are used to provide a uniform level of schooling, it follows immediately from our assumption of logarithmic preferences that all households desire the same tax rate $\tau_t = \delta/(1 + \delta)$. Assume further that government consists of a representative of each of the two groups and that decisions on the orientation of schooling are reached through a bargaining process between them in which the first move is a policy proposal comprising a pair of social orientations—one for schools of the proposer's own constituency and another for those of the rival constituency.

The outcome of the process will then depend on the ability of the first mover to impose its will on the other side. Assume initially that first mover has the coercive power to force the other side to accept its proposal.[12] Then the first mover will select its own social orientation for its own school system and offset the social orientation of the other group to maximize productivity; if, say, the first mover represents the red community, then she will set $p_{rt+1} = p_{rt}$ and $p_{gt+1} = p_{rt} + \Delta$. The equal size of the two groups leads us to assume that each side has an equal probability of being the first mover and so that all parents have the same expected utility.

Comparing welfare levels under this centralized schooling regime to the decentralized regime analyzed in the preceding section, we observe that centralization maximizes children's incomes but inflicts a greater psychic cost on parents. Once adopted, centralized education is clearly preferable to decentralization in all future generations, but for the parent generation making the switch it involves the risk of a greater generation gap than it would have chosen under the decentralized system. This sacrifice is worthwhile—that is, centralization is preferred to decentralization by the parent generation—only if this added psychic cost is outweighed by the material gain to the next generation.[13] A decentralized school system fails to internalize social spillovers and therefore results in an inefficiently high degree of social polarization and a reduced growth rate compared to the social optimum, but a move to coercive centralized education may not produce better results.

At the other extreme, consider a centralized school system in which the first mover has no coercive power. Then, the second mover can reject the first mover's proposal and receive a full tax credit to set up a school system of its own, in which case the two groups revert to the decentralized equilibrium described above. In this case, centralization must perform at least as well as decentralized education. As both groups must agree to the centralized curriculum, expected social polarization in each period can be no greater, and may be smaller, than under decentralization. Thus centralization without coercion is a Pareto improvement over decentralization.

Miguel (2003) compares, empirically, the relative advantages of centralized versus decentralized education systems in the process of nation building, contrasting different education policies in western Kenya and western Tanzania in the postcolonial period. While both regions exhibit much geopolitical similarity and, in particular, a large degree of ethnic fragmentation, their respective national governments pursued very different nation-building strategies. Tanzania was much more aggressive in this regard. It embraced Swahili—seen as ethnically "neutral" in both countries—as the main language of instruction and the official language of government administration. And it adopted a school curriculum stressing a common history, culture, and values and inculcating a sense of national identity from a young age. In contrast, Kenya has not pursued a nation-building policy. Its school curriculum emphasizes the village and the district as opposed to the nation, and local vernaculars, rather than Swahili or English, are used in schools up to the fifth grade, by which time many students drop out of school. Miguel (2003) argues that these policy differences have led to Tanzania investing more in schools (and other local public goods) than Kenya and achieving faster growth rates, leading to the conclusion on empirical grounds that cohesive education policies should figure prominently in the policy agendas of ethnically polarized African countries.

Public Education as a Melting Pot

The previous discussion considered the choice between alternative regimes of public and private education in the context of a symetrically polarized economy. In this section we consider the absorption of a small ethnic minority in the mainstream culture. In immigrant countries such as the United States, public schools have historically enjoyed substantial success in assimilating large immigrant populations. Public education has long been viewed as an "agent of cultural standardization" that draws immigrant children closer to the majority culture by weakening their ties to their parents' traditional values (Katz, 1976). While ethnic and cultural divisions remain a potential source of social tension, the United States continues to be a melting pot in which people from widely varying backgrounds assume a common cultural identity in the course of two or three generations.[14] This success can be at least partly attributed to the method of public finance of education in the United States, which does not reduce the tax liability of parents who opt out of public education, thus requiring them to pay twice if they choose to educate their children privately. This provides strong incentives for minority parents to culturally assimilate their children by sending them to public schools. The greater cultural homogeneity that results has an external beneficial effect on the cultural majority, as it reduces the cost of cultural heterogeneity, which all incur.

We demonstrate these effects by applying the previous analysis of social polarization to the asymmetric interaction between a small immigrant minority and a mainstream majority and by stipulating that tax money can be used only for public education, as it is generally the case in the United States.[15] Public schools, funded by taxes and propagating the values of the cultural majority, then coexist with private schools catering to the needs of those members of the cultural minority who are unwilling to assimilate their children into the mainstream culture.

Consider an economy initially comprising two internally uniform groups: an indigenous, culturally immobile majority and a distinct, potentially assimilating minority. Let w_t denote the measure of the majority in period t, and let $1 - w_t$ denote the measure of the minority.[16] The initial share of the majority w_0 is given and taken to be greater than one half, and this will imply that in subsequent periods $w_{t+1} \geq w_t > \frac{1}{2}$. As before, households are characterized by income and cultural identity. Without loss of generality, we locate the permanent cultural orientation of the majority at the origin and denote by $\Delta_0 > 0$ the uniform initial cultural orientation of the minority; this will imply that future minority cohorts also have a uniform cultural orientation, which we denote Δ_t. Note that the extent of cultural homogeneity in any period t has two dimensions: the larger the size of the majority w_t and the more culturally similar the two groups (that is, the smaller Δ_t is), the more homogeneous is the economy.

The initial distribution of income is given. In subsequent periods, income is produced by parents in proportion to the amount of human capital they acquired as children h_{it}, modified by an exogenous random disturbance term a_{it} and a productivity coefficient Π_{it}, defined similarly to the preceding section as an average of cultural distances.[17] Then $y_{it} = a_{it} h_{it} \Pi_{it}$, where internal cultural uniformity in each group implies that

$$
\Pi_{it} = \begin{cases} w_t + D(\Delta_t)(1 - w_t) \\ \quad \text{if individual } i \text{ belongs to the majority,} \\ w_t D(\Delta_t) + 1 - w_t \\ \quad \text{if individual } i \text{ belongs to the minority.} \end{cases} \tag{8.9}
$$

Both human capital and cultural identity are acquired through education. The amount of human capital accumulated by a child, h_{it+1}, is simply equal to spending per pupil in her school. Her cultural orientation is determined by the type of school she attends. Schooling at a majority-supported school produces a cultural orientation of 0 (the majority cultural orientation), while schooling at a minority-supported school produces a cultural orientation determined by the parents of the children in the school. The cost of schooling is not affected by cultural orientation, and both types of schools are assumed to be equally efficient. Parents make all schooling decisions on behalf of the children, and the utility that the parent of household i in period t maximizes is given by (8.3).

Under decentralized schooling, each parent individually determines the desired amount of human-capital investment in her child (subject to the budget constraint, $y_{it} = c_{it} + h_{it+1}$) and the type of school her child attends—majority supported or minority supported—where minority parents determine the cultural orientation of their schools collectively.[18] Utility maximization by minority parents with respect to cultural orientation balances the tradeoff between parents' desires to share their cultural traditions with their children and concern for their children's material well-being, which is furthered by assimilation in the majority culture.[19]

As in the preceding symmetric analysis of competing ethnic groups, here, too, the equilibrium path is not efficient. Under decentralized schooling, the minority community disregards benefits to the rival community of reducing polarization in making its educational decisions. A Pareto improvement can therefore be achieved through faster cultural assimilation of the minority by minority private schools' adoption of a curriculum closer in its cultural orientation to the mainstream, accompanied by some compensation to minority parents for this move, subsidized by the majority. However, this might be difficult to implement.

Alternatively, the majority can use its political power to achieve a unilateral improvement by creating incentives for more rapid assimilation of the minority. One way of achieving this is through a system of public education in which parents who seek to send their children to private schools are not exempt from paying the education tax. Thus they are required to pay twice for their children's schooling—paying the tax that finances public schools as well as private tuition. We now describe such a system and show that it benefits the majority in two ways: by drawing the minority closer to the mainstream culture and by reducing the tax price of public education.

Consider then an education system in which state schools are funded by a proportional income tax τ_t that is determined by a majority of parents and that is levied on all parents irrespective of the type of school they choose for their children. The revenue raised through the income tax is used to provide a uniform level of schooling for children in public schools. Letting Y_t denote total income in period t, this implies that the amount of human capital accumulated by a child attending a state school is $h_{it+1} = \tau_t Y_t / w_{t+1}$. The amount of private consumption by a household with income y_{it} that sends its child to a state school is $c_{it} = (1 - \tau_t) y_{it}$. Private education is paid for out of after-tax income. To substantially simplify the analysis, suppose that private schools must supply the same quality of education as public schools— that is, they have control only over the cultural orientation of their curriculum, but spending per pupil must be equal in both types of schools. This implies that majority parents will always send their children to public schools.

Suppose that in each period, the majority of parents determine the education tax rate τ_t, anticipating the decisions of the minority. Then each minority parent individually decides whether her child will attend public or private school. Finally, the parents of private-school children collectively determine the cultural orientation of private education. The equilibrium is a sequence of such consistent decisions.

There is then a threshold income level $y(w_{t+1})$ such that all minority parents with income above this threshold send their children to private school, while those with income below it send their children to public school.[20] This is due to the funding structure, as all parents who opt out of public education must pay twice for their children's education, and poorer parents are less able to afford the added expense. As a result, only wealthier parents choose to retain their cultural orientation by sending their children to a private school. We require that in equilibrium parents' anticipations regarding public enrollment are realized. Letting $G_t(y)$ denote the distribution of income in period t among minority parents, $G_t(y(w_{t+1}))$ is the fraction of these parents who send their children to public school. As all majority parents also send their children to public schools, the equilibrium condition is $w_{t+1} = w_t + G_t(y(w_{t+1}))(1 - w_t)$.

Further analysis of this funding regime indicates a dynamic equilibrium path along which the share of public enrollment grows continually while minority schools draw closer to the majority culture. By comparing this funding regime to the decentralized equilibrium, it can be shown that in each period the fraction of the population subscribing to the majority culture, w_t, is higher under public education. Consequently, the cultural distance between the two groups is smaller under public education than under a decentralized school system. Thus public education, so funded, achieves a higher degree of cultural homogeneity than the decentralized school system in both regards. Moreover, it reduces the tax price of public education by a factor of w_{t+1}.[21] For both these reasons it is favored by the cultural majority.

This equilibrium is not fully efficient, however. As private-school parents determine their school curriculum unilaterally, first-order conditions imply that the marginal effect of a small reduction in Δ_{t+1} on minority school parents is negligible. However, the same change will have a nonnegligible benefit for majority parents. It follows that both the minority and the majority can gain from the majority subsidizing private education and the minority aligning the cultural orientation of its schools more closely to the majority culture. This indicates that a coordinated choice of school financing and minority school curriculum content has the potential of making everyone better off, though again implementation of contingent contracts that subsidize private minority schooling in return for changes in the private-school curriculum may be difficult to implement. The notion of centralized state supervision and regulation of private schooling in the United States is possibly as controversial as proposals to use tax-funded vouchers to support religious schools.

Policy Implications

This framework suggests a number of policy implications, which we discuss informally. Gradstein and Justman (2001) extend the above model to study the assimilating effects of public education in the context of immigration. They assume that there is exogenous positive population growth from immigration: in each period new immigrants enter the country with a cultural orientation that is at least as far removed from the mainstream culture as the cultural orientation of the veteran resident minority. This implies that in each period there are three types of parents: majority-culture parents, veteran minority parents, and newcomers. Assume that majority parents determine tax rates (or education quality), that veteran minority parents determine the orientation of minority schools, and that newcomer parents choose only which school their children will attend. The children of newcomers are then no longer newcomers but belong either to the veteran minority or the majority, depending on the school their parents choose for them. The negative effect of polarization on the cultural majority then increases with the size of migration flows but also depends on the income levels of new migrants. Because public schools are available for free while private schools cost money, poor immigrants are more inclined than rich immigrants to send their children to majority-culture public schools that promote their assimilation in the mainstream. Thus, if new immigrants have relatively low incomes, public education is an effective tool of cultural assimilation.

Another application relaxes the assumption that public-school curricula are immobile, ignoring the cultural demands of the minority. The experience of the United States points to various instances in which public schools have accommodated the preferences of immigrant minorities, mostly through bilingual education. Instruction in German was introduced in Ohio as early as 1839, despite occasional setbacks spread widely, especially in the Midwest, and continued throughout the nineteenth and early twentieth centuries. This trend was reversed in the early twentieth century as anti-German sentiment in the wake of World War I led to the dismantling of all bilingual education by the 1920s. More recently, the large influx of Spanish-speaking immigrants spurred a revival of bilingual education, initially among Cuban immigrants in Florida in the early 1960s and later in Texas, California, and others states; and again a backlash has recently led voters in California and Arizona to approve measures that eliminate bilingual education in their states.

To incorporate this in the model, Gradstein and Justman (2001) allows the cultural orientation of public schools in each period to be endogenously determined by majority parents, along with the education tax rate. Such cultural accommodation reduces average social distance in the next generation, thereby potentially increasing productivity. Their analysis indicates that the introduction of multicultural elements in public-school curricula by way of moving the cultural orientation of public schools closer to the minority-cultural orientation is more likely when the share of the minority is small. Combining this with the effect of immigration, discussed in the preceding paragraph, this suggests that as increased migration allows minority groups to gain political influence in the school districts in which they are concentrated and to use this influence to strengthen bilingual education in the public schools, broader forces at the state and federal levels may then work to curtail these initiatives.

Finally, the above analysis has implications for the debate on education vouchers, discussed in chapter 7. While the earlier analysis in this chapter suggests that contingent contracts, which regulate school curricula, have welfare-enhancing potential, it also pointed out the difficulties of implementation. It is possible, however, that subsidizing private education—through tuition tax credits, education vouchers, or direct defraying of some of the costs of private education—may be desirable for the majority and hence a Pareto improvement, even without a reciprocal change in the cultural orientation of minority schooling. Specifically, the cultural majority can subsidize those parents who choose to opt out of the public-school system and send their children to a private school. Such a subsidy reduces the tax price of education spending and can thus increase spending per pupil in the public system provided private enrollment is sufficiently elastic with respect to the rate of subsidization and subsidies are targeted at parents who would not otherwise choose private education. Indeed, previous analyses have argued that such an increase is indicated for typical parameter values that prevail in the United States.[22] If this were the only consideration, such a subsidy would be a Pareto improvement, and we would expect to see broader popular support for school vouchers than is actually observed. That they are not—even limited, experimental school voucher programs are hotly contested—suggests that any fiscal benefits are outweighed by the detrimental effect of increased private enrollment on cultural homogeneity. The analysis in Gradstein and Justman (2001) highlights this detrimental effect that subsidizing private education has in increasing cultural polarization. Vouchers or other forms of private-school subsidies can expect to find broad popular support only when the cost of increased polarization is small and outweighed by other benefits of subsidized private schooling.

Conclusions

This chapter focuses on aspects of education less commonly addressed in formal economic analyses: its role as a socializing force. That education plays an important role in this regard is widely accepted by both students and practitioners of education, and here we consider its material consequences, in the context of parental decisions that trade off the intrinsic value of retaining a traditional cultural against the material benefits of a mainstream education, as these decisions bear on the aggregate well-being of the economy.

These features introduce novel considerations in the comparison between education systems. Decentralized schooling tends to generate a more diverse set of social values, possibly leading to excessive social polarization. In contrast, public schooling is perceived as offering a more uniform curriculum that promotes assimilation of minority cultures but may be excessively homogeneous for some minority parents. This approach is consistent with the traditional view of public education as a melting pot, which promotes social cohesion among individuals with widely diverse backgrounds. While decentralization results in too much polarization and public education in excessive homogenization, the presented analysis suggests that a fully efficient education system may be difficult to implement.

Education funding in the United States, which requires minority parents to pay twice for private schools that educate their children in traditional minority cultural values, provides a strong incentive for rapid assimilation, especially for the assimilation of poorer immigrants, and reduces the tax price of public education. Tax-funded education vouchers ease the financial burden of private education and may have a favorable fiscal impact on the majority as well but may also promote social polarization. Their net effect on welfare depends on the tradeoff between these two factors. Multiculturalism in public education increases minority participation in public schools while allowing some retention of cultural identity, suggesting that it is more likely to be supported by the majority when the minority group is small.

9   Directions for Future Research

Thou shalt not do as the dean pleases, Thou shalt not write thy doctor's thesis
  On education.

—W. H. Auden, "Under Which Lyre" (1946)

In modern industrialized countries, elementary and secondary education is financed and controlled largely by the public sector and therefore partly shaped by the political aggregation of popular sentiment. These public systems of education often allow households to choose among autonomous public schools or publicly funded private schools or to opt out of the system. Thus households act in these systems both as political entities that shape public education policies through the ballot box and also as individual decision makers who are realizing their preferences within the constraints of the public policies chosen through the political process.

This interaction between the ballot box and the marketplace in education systems that combine public and private dimensions provides a rich field of inquiry. Education is an important driver of economic growth and a key determinant of the distribution of material resources, as well as a strong cultural force. Forming effective policies for the development and reform of education systems requires an understanding of the links between the political and economic organization of education and the economic and social variables that it affects. The challenging theoretical problems it raises are not only of keen interest in themselves but also bear a more general relevance for the functioning of modern mixed economies.

In this volume we have shown how simple formal models that incorporate political decisions in economic analyses of growth, distribution, location, and school choice can be used to illustrate the underlying economic principles that shape the functioning of public education. Such models highlight the tradeoffs implicit in the choice of education systems and provide a basic framework for policy analysis, though they are rarely sufficient in themselves to serve as operational guides to policy. Specific policy recommendations require more detailed modeling, beyond the scope of the present volume, to capture the particular circumstances of concrete issues. This offers many avenues for further research.

One such avenue concerns the effect of political factors on the efficiency of public education. While much research has focused on the political determination of the level of spending on public education, a similar conceptual effort is needed to understand the political forces that shape its efficiency. Inadequate governance due to imperfect monitoring and weak accountability in public systems, frequently cited as a source of inefficiency in public schools, may be alleviated by the competitive forces of school choice or by closer external monitoring of education outcomes. Proponents present empirical evidence that competitive pressure does indeed improve performance in public schools and see external testing as a necessary concomitant of decentralization. Critics warn of the wasteful effort of "teaching to the test," a theme amplified in a recent contribution by Acemoglu et al. (2003). Given the difficulty of measuring educational output, excessive competition may induce wasteful signaling efforts on the part of schools and teachers. Initiatives to reform public education by allowing for more choice among publicly funded schooling options combined with closer monitoring of school performance must address these issues in a political context. The incentives that clearly play an important role in determining the efficiency of education systems are still not well understood; and even less do we understand the positive political economy that shapes them.

Another dimension of education that merits further theoretical analysis is the political economy of education as a signaling mechanism, as distinct from its role in building human capital. This relates in the first instance to earmarking successful students at an early age—and thus significantly increasing their chances of success. Similar effects arise with regard to graduation. Predicating graduation on passing a selective, external examination—"high-stakes" testing—has very different signaling implications from allowing high schools to award diplomas at their sole discretion. Decisions on screening, streaming, and graduation criteria in public education can have very different effects on different households and are invariably made in a political context.

Adding institutional detail to the political framework of the analysis offers yet another direction for further research. Existing models generally cast voters as similar consumers of education—often ignoring differences between households in ages, family size, religion, or home ownership—and often overlook the effect of specific voting procedures on political outcomes (Romer and Rosenthal, 1978). Substantial progress has been achieved in incorporating some of these dimensions in models that combine decisions on residential location, school choice, and the division of public education financing between local and state jurisdictions (Nechyba, 2000; Epple and Sieg, 1999), but more remains to be done, especially in extending these models dynamically, to assess their long-term implications.

Finally, most analyses focus on the demand for education while ignoring the specific conditions of its supply. Both positive and normative analyses of decentralization and privatization of public education systems depend very much on the response of private-sector education entrepreneurs to proposed reforms, as well as on the supply of school administrators and teachers. These will be strongly affected by political and institutional factors—not only local, state, and federal government but also notably teachers' unions and religious organizations.

These and other directions for future research on the political economy of education highlight both the intellectual challenges it offers and its great practical importance.

Notes

Chapter 1

1. Schultz (1963, 1971) and Becker (1993/1964) are seminal references on education as investment in human capital.

2. For seminal expositions of the screening theory of education, see Arrow (1973), Spence (1973), and Stiglitz (1975).

3. An early contribution to the literature on social capital is Adelman and Morris (1967). Its recent currency owes much to Putnam's (1993) influential essay.

4. The role of screening is more pronounced in tertiary education (Arrow, 1973).

5. See Loury (1981) for an early exposition of this point and Banerjee and Newman (1993) and Galor and Zeira (1993) for more recent work along these lines. We expand on this in chapter 5. Heckman (2000) and Cameron and Heckman (2001) argue that liquidity constraints are empirically significant only at early stages of education.

6. Arguing from equity considerations that provision of certain goods and services should not depend on the marketplace is often referred to as *specific egalitarianism*. See also Tobin (1970).

7. See Arrow (1971), Bruno (1976), and Ulph (1977) for formal analyses of this argument.

8. See Herrnstein and Murray (1994) for a controversial view of this issue that stresses the importance of innate abilities, and see critical responses by Heckman (1995) and Ashenfelter and Rouse (2000), among many others.

9. Lott (1990, 1999) and Pritchett (2003) emphasize the use of public education by ruling regimes as an instrument of control. Gradstein and Justman (2000, 2002) highlight its role in promoting social cohesion. We elaborate on this in chapter 8.

Chapter 2

1. The education of the guardians was meant to instill in them a combination of fighting spirit toward the enemies of the Republic and kindness toward its citizens (*The Republic*, bk. 2). Rousseau (1979/1762, p. 40) thought Plato's *Republic* "the most beautiful educational treatise ever written."

2. Babylonian Talmud, Baba Batra 21:1. This is the source of the "Maimonides rule," to which Angrist and Lavy (1999) refer, which requires that class size not exceed forty pupils. Another issue that the Talmud discusses is whether teachers who cover more material but make mistakes should be preferred to slower but more careful teachers. The implicit answer is that they should exercise great care, as even small mistakes can have grave consequences.

3. Martin Luther urged state involvement in education and, in particular, enactment of compulsory schooling laws.

4. Rousseau's enormously influential treatise on education, *Emile*, emphasized the role of education in reconciling natural self-esteem with the need to live among others in a civil society—to be both man and citizen.

5. Beccaria's *Tratto dei delitti e delle pene* (1764), which advocated the prevention of crime through education, is cited by Finer (1997, p. 1437) as having had "an enormous impact on the enlightened monarchs."

6. Empress Maria-Theresa of Austro-Hungary established a comprehensive system of education through the General Education Regulation of 1774, and by the end of her reign there were in her hereditary lands 3,848 elementary schools, 83 high schools, and 15 teacher-training colleges serving over 200,000 pupils (Finer, 1997, bk. 4, ch. 8, p. 1453).

7. Tertiary education also developed in this period. The University of Berlin was founded in 1810, and the state nationalized the autonomous universities in its territory in 1817.

8. The United States first established a separate cabinet-level Department of Education in 1980, and to this day federal funds account for only 7 percent of elementary and secondary school spending.

9. The first state board of education was established in Massachusetts in 1837.

10. Kindergartens were incorporated in the public school system toward the end of the nineteenth century.

11. The expansion of higher education dates to the second half of the twentieth century, spurred by the GI Bill, which offered World War II veterans a free college education. As Goldin (1998) emphasizes, this could not have been possible without the prior spread of high school education. Federal support for tertiary education is proportionally more extensive than at lower levels, beginning with the Morrill Land Grant Act of 1862 that gave each of the states federal land to support at least one college, with the main objective of teaching "branches of learning as related to agriculture and mechanical arts." Thus at the tertiary level, too, American education was more egalitarian than its European counterparts of the time.

12. Major efforts are also directed to making tertiary schooling widely available by establishing systems of public universities, mainly financed through taxes, and by providing state-backed education loans. Public universities produce the vast majority of university graduates in Europe and a smaller majority of graduates in the United States.

13. Of course, administrative control will also vary from country to country in a manner that may not be reflected in funding patterns.

14. In this Germany differs from other European countries, such as France and Italy, where education is primarily the responsibility of the central government.

15. For a theoretical analysis of the evolution of a hierarchical differentiation between vocational and general education, see Bertocchi and Spagat (2004). At the tertiary level, about 2 percent of public expenditure is directed to government-dependent private institutions. Tuition fees in the public universities are virtually nonexistent, and a significant fraction of university students are eligible for means-tested benefits to cover living expenses.

16. In the early 1990s, the highest-spending state (excluding Alaska) spent over three times as much per student as the lowest-spending state; at the end of the decade, this ratio declined to 2.5. This comparison does not take into account differences in factor costs across states.

17. At the tertiary level, private sources provide approximately 75 percent of funds.

18. Other agencies are responsible for on-the-job training, special education, early childhood development, and career services.

19. About two thirds of the student population is of European descent, 20 percent are Maori, and the remainder is about equally divided between other Pacific Islanders and Asians.

Chapter 3

1. To reconcile increasing aggregate returns to education with decreasing individual returns, endogenous growth models must assume that external benefits from education raise social returns above private returns.

2. The argument follows from a view of development as transition from an agrarian to an industrialized society through an intermediate phase in which the two exist simultaneously as a *dual economy*. A simple formal argument runs as follows: Assume that income per capita is uniformly w_a in the agrarian sector and w_i in the industrialized sector and that q is the share of the industrialized sector in the labor force. Then the variance of income, as a measure of inequality, is $q(1 - q)(w_i - w_a)^2$, which is an inverse U-shaped function of q maximized at $q = \frac{1}{2}$. See Lindert and Williamson (1985) for a summary of historical evidence on the Kuznets curve.

3. We discuss their model in detail in chapter 5.

4. This macroeconomic approach ignores the important affect of microeconomic institutional arrangements. Social mobility and inequality are strongly affected by the manner in which education is financed, by the extent to which students are sorted through schools' admissions policies and by streaming, and so on. Of course, these arrangements are also influenced by political factors and hence by the distribution of income, which affects the distribution of political power, but other independent factors—historical rigidities, cultural mores—are also at work here. We return to the connection between education finance and income distribution in subsequent chapters.

5. This is not a source of bias in measuring private returns if ability cannot be identified except through education, functioning as a screening mechanism. There are also countervailing biases, notably the omission of nonmonetary effects such as the consumption value of education, the pleasure (or pain!) of learning, or the psychological advantages of an interesting job. The benefits of an education are underestimated also if self-selection implies that graduates are especially inept at the mechanical jobs that would be open to them if they did not have a degree (Willis and Rosen, 1979).

6. Various methodological issues bear on the empirical analysis. The rate of accumulation of human capital is typically measured as current investment in schooling, often proxied by the high school enrollment rate. But a large part of investment in education takes the form of the forgone labor earnings of students, which vary directly with the level of their human-capital investment. And some education—in philosophy, religion, or literature—is pursued for its own sake and not as a means of accumulating economically productive human capital.

7. The three subsamples are ninety-eight "nonoil" countries (excluding oil producers), seventy-five intermediate countries (excluding also very small countries), and twenty-two OECD countries. The model was least successful in explaining variance in output levels among OECD countries but more successful in explaining variance in growth rates among these countries.

8. The internal rates of return are calculated as follows: For an elasticity of 0.80, an increase of, say, 10 percent in education spending amounts to an extra 1 percent of GDP spent on education and generates an increase of 8 percent in steady-state output, which, spread out over forty years, gives an annual increase of 0.2 percent. An internal rate of return of 20 percent equates the present value of the constant forty-year negative flow of 1 percent of GDP and an increasing positive flow of 0.2, 0.4, 0.6, 0.8, . . . , 8 percent.

9. While Barro (1991) fails to detect a significant relationship between primary schooling and growth, primary schooling is a prerequisite for training at higher levels.

10. In related work, Bils and Klenow (2000) test for the direction of causality between human-capital accumulation and growth, concluding that the direction of causality is most likely to be the reverse, growth causing human-capital accumulation. Cohen and Soto (2001) present a dissenting view using a different data set.

11. This assumes fertility and schooling are jointly determined (see, e.g., Becker et al., 1990).

12. The large body of empirical research on mobility carried out by sociologists, constituting the large majority of work on this topic, is generally not linked to economic models and represents for economists an untapped reservoir of knowledge on the subject. See, for example, Erikson and Goldthorpe (1993) for a comparative empirical analysis of various dimensions of social mobility after World War II in a selection of European countries, the United States, Australia, and Japan.

13. $2^{0.4} = 1.32$ while $2^{0.2} = 1.15$; and $(2^{0.4})^{0.4} = 1.12$ while $(2^{0.2})^{0.2} = 1.03$.

Chapter 4

1. This assumption is consistent with actual income distributions; cf. Neal and Rosen (2000) among many others.

2. This intertemporal utility specification is sometimes referred to as the "warm glow" motive for parental altruism (Andreoni, 1989). Its main virtue relative to full dynastic altruism, whereby parents' utility depends on all their descendants' utilities, is simplicity. This is especially important in the context of voting on public education, where dynastic specification may lead to intractable formulations.

3. A concave production function (with declining marginal productivity) is introduced in the next chapter, where we imbed the model in a dynamic setting and consider its

behavior in the steady state. For present purposes, assuming linear production does not substantively affect our results.

4. It obviously matters how the education budget is spent. Spending aimed at increasing the number of years at school appears to be more effective than money invested in school buildings; money spent on remedial education in lower elementary grades has been shown to be more effective than money spent at later ages; and so on. See chapter 3's Resources and Schooling section above for further discussion and references.

5. The elasticity of substitution between consumption and schooling is the inverse of the elasticity of the marginal rate of substitution U_c/U_s with respect to c/s in absolute value or, equivalently, the elasticity of the chosen value of c/s with respect to the price ratio p_c/p_s in absolute value: the percent change in c/s caused by a 1 percent change in p_c/p_s.

6. This abstracts from the precise nature of the tax base for financing public education. In the United States, for example, local property taxes and sales taxes levied by the states account for a majority of public spending on education. Our simplified analysis implicitly assumes a strong correlation between income and these other tax bases.

7. This follows seminal analyses of voting equilibria by Stiglitz (1974) and Usher (1977).

8. If, for example, there are three households, A, B, and C, each with single-peaked preferences, and A's most preferred tax rate is 10 percent, B's is 18 percent, and C's is 16 percent, then 16 percent is a political equilibrium: it commands a majority over any other tax rate in pairwise comparison. In the appendix to this chapter, we review the conditions for the existence of voting equilibria.

9. From (4.8a), the chosen tax rate is $\tau^* = \delta/[(Y/y_m)^{1-\sigma}\delta^{1-\sigma} + \delta]$, and Y/y_m is the ratio of mean to median income.

10. Bergstrom et al. (1982, model 4) found an elasticity of -0.05; Rubinfeld et al. (1987), controlling for Tiebout sorting, found an elasticity of -0.01; and Rubinfeld and Shapiro (1989, model B) found an elasticity of 0.011. In all cases, the size of the net effect was less than one standard deviation in both the income and price coefficients.

11. In the preceding chapter we cite work by Heckman (2000) and Carneiro et al. (2003) on the importance of early education, showing that the cost effectiveness of education intervention decreases strongly with age.

12. In chapter 1 we cite Herrnstein and Murray's (1994) controversial work on the genetic transmission of abilities and opposing views.

13. Glomm and Ravikumar (1992), Gradstein and Justman (1997), and Bénabou (1996c, 2000) are some recent contributions that examine the choice between education systems from a political economy perspective.

14. When the elasticity of substitution does not equal one, the comparison of utility levels is less straightforward. The median voter obtains the same level of education under public schooling as under private schooling but pays less for it and therefore prefers public to private schooling, and the same will apply to households earning close to median income. Voters earning above-average income clearly prefer private education, as it would enable them to obtain the same level of education as under public education but at a lower price. However, other households may not prefer public schooling, as it allows them to pay less for the education they are getting but does not provide them with the amount of education they want.

15. In Justman and Gradstein (1999), we show that the Education Acts that made schooling compulsory and later free in nineteenth-century Britain were enacted shortly after extension of the franchise lowered the income of the median enfranchised household below average income. We expand on this in chapter 5.

16. Production externalities may be more significant at low schooling levels, which promote basic communication and technical skills.

17. We expand on both these issues—the relative efficiency of public and private schooling and the religious factor in education—in chapter 7.

18. This assumption can be justified by appealing to productivity losses resulting from an excessively high tax rate (Gradstein, 2000); such productivity losses are more fully incorporated in Perotti (1993).

19. Continuity of preferences ensures that the same arguments apply when the redistribution parameter is sufficiently close to one.

20. Their emphasis is on extension of the political franchise, but mass education could also serve as a means of alleviating redistributive tension.

Chapter 5

1. Our exposition of these issues follows the seminal work of Loury (1981) and later contributions by Aghion and Bolton (1997), Banerjee and Newman (1993), Galor and Zeira (1993), Piketty (1997), and Gradstein and Justman (1997).

2. In subsequent chapters we introduce additional dimensions of diversity in the population.

3. Earlier work by Stiglitz (1969) and Bourguignon (1981) pointed out the significance of convexity of the production function for balanced growth and distribution assuming exogenous investment behavior.

4. The assumption of imperfect credit markets, implying self-financing of education, is crucial in this context; with perfect credit markets all families could invest the minimal amount needed. However, as several authors have shown in related contexts (e.g., Piketty, 1997; Aghion and Bolton, 1997; Banerjee and Newman, 1993), the nonconvexity assumption is not essential for generating poverty and low mobility traps. Paying detailed attention to the functioning of endogenized credit markets, they show that such traps may arise if moral hazard renders the risks of investment in human capital uninsurable.

5. This was suggested by Romer (1986) in a representative agent model. Gradstein and Justman (1997) consider the efficiency of education subsidies with a heterogeneous population.

6. This follows Loury's (1981) seminal work. Recent extensions of Loury's framework that explicitly incorporate growth issues include Owen and Weil (1998), Maoz and Moav (1999), and Hassler and Mora (2000).

7. The role of direct parental input in the accumulation of human capital is discussed further in chapter 4.

8. In this specification, if $\alpha < 1$ and γ is less than one third, public schooling achieves higher long-run average income independently of the value of α. In the limiting case of

$\alpha = 1$, the economy grows endogenously in the steady state, and as the marginal productivity of schooling is uniform across households, there is always less steady-state growth under public education than under private education.

9. These two conditions are equivalent for a lognormal distribution.

10. The assumption of logarithmic utility contributes to this conclusion, as it implies that all households desire the same tax level, an assumption that may be a reasonable approximation for local communities (Cohen-Zada and Justman, 2003). However, under other utility functions preferences vary, and the advantages of progressive redistribution for the poor may be outweighed by the disadvantage of a tax rate that may be higher or lower than the tax rate they prefer.

11. For empirical evidence on the propensity to vote as an increasing function of income (and education), see the early summary of Verba et al. (1978), as well as Ashenfelter and Kelley (1975), Filer et al. (1991), and Brady et al. (1995), among others.

12. The first Education Act of 1870 followed the substantial extension of the franchise through the Second Reform Act of 1867, which tipped the income of the median enfranchised voter above average income (Justman and Gradstein, 1999). The Third Reform Act of 1882–1884, which further extended the franchise, was followed by further legislation that extended publicly funded education (Dicey, 1962/1914).

13. As Adam Smith (1976/1776, bk. 5, ch. 1, pt. 3, art. 2) wrote a century earlier, "An instructed and intelligent people, besides, are always more decent and orderly than an ignorant and stupid one.... They are more disposed to examine, and more capable of seeing through, the interested complaints of faction and sedition, and they are, upon that account, less apt to be misled into any wanton or unnecessary opposition to the measures of government."

14. In each period t we have $\psi_t^2 = \gamma^{2t}\psi_0^2 + (1 - \gamma^{2t})(1 - \gamma)\varepsilon^2/(1 + \gamma)$. See Aitchison and Brown (1969) for an analysis of the general properties of the lognormal distribution.

15. $\theta_t = \text{Cov}(\ln(y_{it}), \ln(a_{it})) = \text{Cov}(\ln(a_{it}) + \alpha \ln(y_{it-1}), \ln(a_{it})) = \text{Var}(\ln(a_{it})) + \text{Cov}(\alpha \ln \cdot (y_{it-1}), \gamma \ln(a_{it-1}) + (1-\gamma) \ln(b_{it})) = \psi_t^2 + \alpha\gamma\theta_{t-1} = \gamma^{2t}\psi_0^2 + (1 - \gamma^{2t})(1 - \gamma)\varepsilon^2/(1 + \gamma) + \alpha\gamma\theta_{t-1}$.

16. To simplify the analysis we stipulate a fixed exogenous franchise requirement. In Justman and Gradstein (1999), the franchise requirement is endogenously determined by the electorate in each period. This accelerates the expansion of the electorate, which grows both because incomes are rising and because the franchise requirement falls, as a result of the expanding electorate. The analysis could be formulated in terms of an education requirement for voting without changing the gist of the argument.

17. With logarithmic utilities, consumption is the same for each household under both private and public education regimes, but the education differential is an increasing function of income. Only the average-income household has the same amount of education under both regimes.

18. $F_t(y_{dt}) = F_t(\hat{y}) + \frac{1}{2} = \Phi[(\ln \hat{y} - \mu_t)/\sigma_t] + \frac{1}{2}; F_t(Y_t) = \Phi[(\mu_t + \frac{1}{2}\sigma_t^2 - \mu_t)/\sigma_t] = \Phi[\frac{1}{2}\sigma_t]$.

Chapter 6

1. In the United States and Germany, individual states assume primary responsibility for education, with the federal government providing less than 10 percent of education spending. In contrast, in Italy and France, the national government is predominant in

financing public education. When we refer to a central government, we have in mind the supralocal political entity—a state in the United States, the nation in France—that assumes primary responsibility for education.

2. See Murray, Evans, and Schwab (1998) and Downes and Figlio (1999) for broad evaluations of these reforms.

3. In chapter 7 we consider the implications of school choice for residential location.

4. The model can easily be extended to any number of income groups and school districts, as long as there are at least as many districts as income groups.

5. There is also a continuum of unstable symmetric equilibria in which the two districts, though varying in size, have the same minority fraction of rich individuals in the population. The tax rate, chosen by the poor, is then identical in both districts. These equilibria are not stable because if a rich household relocates from district a to b, then school spending in district b increases (as the tax rate does not change), creating an incentive for additional migration to district b.

6. Of course, this might not be the case if inferior schooling in the poorer district generated negative externalities, such as crime, for the richer district.

7. In the next chapter we consider the interaction of residential location and local public schooling when there is variation in local incomes.

8. This abstracts from specific aspects of actual tax funding of public schooling. In many European countries, progressive—rather than proportional—general tax revenues fund public education. In the United States, most local revenues for funding education derive from property taxes, and while property values are correlated with income, they also reflect additional factors. We ignore this distinction for the moment.

9. Of course, as a practical matter uniform spending does not imply uniform quality of schooling. School outcomes can be enhanced through added private spending on education and are affected by conditions in the home that reflect economic resources, cultural mores, family values, and so on, all of which are amplified by peer-group effects. Consequently, equalizing education spending, while diminishing the correlation between education outcomes and parental socioeconomic status, does not eliminate it.

10. We assume that poorer districts face constraints in long-term borrowing similar to those faced by low-income households.

11. However, some European countries, such as Belgium or the Netherlands, rely almost exclusively on state finance, as do some states in the United States (Hawaii is an extreme example). For a useful survey of the extensive empirical literature on the substitution between state and local spending in the United States, in a variety of contexts, see Hines and Thaler (1995).

12. When $\tau = 0$, this is equivalent to pure local financing.

13. Districts with exactly average income are indifferent between the two.

14. This conclusion does not depend on the homogeneity of local communities. For a household with income Y_{ij} the local tax price Y_{ij}/Y_j is less than the central tax price Y_{ij}/Y if and only if $Y_j > Y$.

15. See Epple and Romano (1996b) for further details.

16. The median preferred tax rate is not necessarily the tax rate preferred by the median-income household, as we show immediately.

17. Under the assumption that median income is less than average income, Y_d must also be less than average income. Districts with above-average income that prefer no foundation grant at all join forces with low-income districts that prefer a lower grant. The median preferred grant level is therefore that of a district with no more than median income. We expand on this below.

18. The foundation level of education spending is $\tau_f Y$, and this is also what it costs under pure local finance. Under a foundation system, residents of district j pay $\tau_f Y_j$ for this level of schooling, which is less than $\tau_f Y$ for districts with below-average income and more for those with above-average income.

19. Stigler (1970) referred to this type of political alignment as "Director's law." The coalition for smaller foundation grants comprises the $1 - F(Y)$ richer districts with greater than average income and the $F(Y_d)$ poorer districts earning less than Y_d.

20. Assume two districts with incomes $Y_1 > Y_2$ and education spending s_1 and s_2, and consider how the spending ratio s_1/s_2 is affected by a marginal increase in the foundation grant. If neither district supplements the grant before the increase, then it will surely not do so after the increase, which leaves s_1/s_2 unchanged. If district 1 supplements the grant before the increase and district 2 does not, increasing the size of the grant increases s_2 while decreasing district 1's supplement, which implies a decline in s_1/s_2. Finally, assume both districts supplement schooling before the increase. Then an increase in the foundation grant gives both the same amount of extra schooling at greater cost to the richer district, causing the richer district to scale back its supplementary spending more than the poorer district.

21. They apply their model to the provision of health services, but their analysis is directly applicable, with small modifications, to local education financing supplementing a central foundation grant. See also Gouveia (1997) and Gradstein and Justman (1996) for related analyses.

Chapter 7

1. That privately operated schools are more efficient than public schools has been presented as a central a priori argument for vouchers, at least since Adam Smith (1976/1776, bk. 5, ch. 1, art. 2), who emphasized the importance of "the master being partly, but not wholly, paid by the public, because, if he was wholly, or even principally, paid by it, he would soon learn to neglect his business," a view shared by Thomas Paine (1984/1792, pt. 2) and revived by Friedman (1962). Theoretical analysis points out that where the supply of private schools is not fully competititve—because of scale effects or differentiation—tuition may be marked up above marginal cost, and the quality of education may not be socially optimal (cf. Spence, 1975). There is some evidence that Catholic schools, despite their lower costs, achieve better academic results than public schools (Evans and Schwab, 1995; Neal, 1997; Sander, 1997). A recent study of nonacademic outcomes found no evidence that a Catholic education reduces risky behavior among teenagers (Mocan et al., 2002). Comparing efficiency across different school types is conceptually difficult because of the multidimensional nature of school quality and raises methodological challenges in controlling for the quality of incoming pupils. Belfield and Levin's (2002, p. 279) review of the empirical evidence on the effects of private

competition on the efficiency of public schools finds "positive gains from competition that are modest in scope with respect to feasible changes in levels of competition," while cautioning "on the validity of inference from point estimates to public policy."

2. Levin and Driver (1997, p. 277) itemize the information costs of voucher programs, noting that in past school-choice programs "non-white and low-income parents had less information than white and middle-income parents."

3. Local schools can also serve as focal points for communal activity, especially in suburban communities (Fischel, 2002).

4. See Levin and Driver (1997) for a careful account of the costs of voucher programs. While it seems possible to design a voucher scheme that is not a burden on the public purse—we consider this in some detail later in the chapter—the costs of the program are immediate while the savings generated by students leaving the public system materialize only gradually.

5. Chubb and Moe (1990) played an influential role in this revival.

6. In a five-to-four decision, the Court determined that the program was not in violation of the Establishment Clause of the First Amendment because it "was enacted for the valid secular purpose of providing educational assistance to poor children in a demonstrably failing public school system" and "is neutral with respect to religion and provides assistance directly to a broad class of citizens who, in turn, direct government aid to religious schools wholly as a result of their own genuine and independent private choice." The dissenting opinions expressed concern for he damage that might be done to the fabric of society by this decision. In Justice Stevens's words, "Whenever we remove a brick from the wall that was designed to separate religion and government, we increase the risk of religious strife and weaken the foundation of our democracy."

7. In 2000, voucher initiatives were defeated in referenda in California and Michigan.

8. The National Center for Education Statistics has estimated that approximately 25 percent of K–12 students in the United States did not attend neighborhood schools in 1999–2000.

9. Surveys by Ladd (2002) and Neal (2002) summarize the varied experience with school choice from different perspectives. See also Howell et al. (2002) for a comprehensive review and analysis of the empirical evidence from randomized field trials in the United States.

10. Thus we ignore the possibility of privately supplementing public education. We also assume for the moment that the structure of the local community is exogenous. Residential location effects, considered separately from school choice in chapter 6, are integrated in our current model later in the chapter. This modeling approach follows Rangazas (1995b), Epple and Romano (1996a), and Glomm and Ravikumar (1998), among others.

11. We discuss the impact of material resources on the quality of education in chapters 3 and 4, but for our current purpose it is sufficient that parents equate higher spending per student with quality. We ignore peer-group effects for the moment (Epple and Romano, 1998), incorporating them later in the chapter when we consider the interaction between school choice and residential location.

12. This formulation ignores religious differentiation and the fixed costs of education, which imply that the variety of private education in smaller communities is limited.

13. $V(\tau, q^e, y_i) = [(1 - \tau)y_i]^{(1-1/\sigma)}/(1 - 1/\sigma) + \delta[\tau Y/q^e]^{(1-1/\sigma)}/(1 - 1/\sigma)$.

14. We assume here for simplicity that all parents share the same perception. Later in the chapter we allow variation in the subjective valuation of private education.

15. This abstracts from the indirect effect of public schooling on crime rates, property values, and so on, which might raise the preferred tax rate. For our purpose it is sufficient that these households prefer lower tax rates than the tax rate that is actually chosen. Considerations such as these enter explicitly in the analysis when a housing market is introduced in the model.

16. As we show in the next section, this segregation by income does not hold when there is innate variation among households in the utility they derive from education, for religious or other reasons (Epple and Sieg, 1999). Of course, private enrollment is also affected by the local *supply* of private education—shaped by scale, density, religious affiliation, and so on—as empirical studies show.

17. See the appendix to chapter 4 for a discussion of conditions for existence of a political equilibrium.

18. This is the equilibrium posited by Sonstelie (1982), Rangazas (1995b), and Epple and Romano (1996a), among others.

19. The size of the coalition for a lower tax rate is $F(y_d)$ (the poor) $+ 1 - q$ (the rich), and this must equal 0.5 if household d is decisive, which gives (7.2b). Epple and Romano (1996a) show this to be sufficient for a local equilibrium, pointing out that institutional restrictions that set a minimal threshold for public spending may rule out rival equilibria. Nechyba (2000) makes the point that if parents choose the type of school their children attend *before* they vote on the tax rate, then voting preferences are single-peaked, and existence holds in any case.

20. In 1997–98, 5,076,119 students were enrolled in private schools in the United States, about 10 percent of total K–12 enrollment. Of these, 2,514,699 attended Catholic schools, and 1,764,447 attended other religious private schools, together accounting for 84.2 percent of total private enrollment (National Center for Education Statistics, 2000, table 60). Econometric estimates of the demand for private schooling in the United States and other countries consistently attribute a prominent role to religious factors (Clotfelter, 1976; James, 1987; Buddin et al., 1998; among others).

21. In 1993–94 in the United States, average tuition was $1,628 in Catholic elementary schools, $2,606 in other religious elementary schools, and $4,693 in nonsectarian private elementary schools. In secondary education, average tuition was $3,643 in Catholic schools, $5,261 in other religious schools, and $9,525 in nonsectarian private schools. Overall, average tuition was $2,178 in Catholic schools, $2,915 in other religious schools, and $6,631 in nonsectarian private schools, compared to average current expenditures of $5,327 per pupil in fall enrollment in public elementary and secondary schools (National Center for Education Statistics, 2000, tables 62, 170). Hoxby (1998) estimates that charitable subsidies from all sources reduce tuition costs in religious schools by as much as 50 percent. Catholic elementary schools received 24.1 percent of their revenues from parish subsidies in 2000–01, and average salaries received by religious sisters serving as principals in these schools were 60 percent lower than those of public school principals (National Catholic Educational Association, 2001, cited in *Zelman v. Simmons-Harris*, fn. 15). However, tuition may not fully reflect private costs if parents are expected to supplement it with donations of their own time or money, as is often the case in religious schools, suggesting that actual subsidies may be less than 50 percent. The effect of such subsidies

on enrollment is evident from the Cleveland voucher program, where a large fraction of participating families were Baptists who sent their children to Catholic schools.

22. This is evident from the large majority of children in Catholic schools who come from Catholic homes (87.9 percent nationwide in 1989–90; National Catholic Educational Association, 1990), which indicates that while attending a Catholic school may improve academic achievement to some degree (see note 1 above), the qualities that parents seek in these schools have a predominantly religious dimension. Instruction in the Catholic faith, which these schools offer, is an important positive factor for many of these parents—and an overriding negative factor for many non-Catholics parents.

23. Until the recent U.S. Supreme Court decision in *Zelman v. Simmons-Harris*, it was widely assumed that the constitutional separation of church and state categorically excluded any such support. See also note 6, above.

24. The model described here follows Cohen-Zada and Justman (2002). The parameter z_i is implicitly defined in relation to the local supply of private religious schools. Thus in a school district in which all religious schools are Catholic, all Jewish parents might have z values well below one, while if there were Jewish private schools in the area, some would have z values greater than one. A natural extension of the model would allow multiple religious groups and an endogenous supply of religious schooling for each group. Cohen-Zada (2002) introduces peer-group effects in the transmission of religious values.

25. Epple et al. (1984), Epple and Romer (1991), and Epple and Sieg (1999) analyze general models of voting and location. Rangazas (1995b) applies his approach to calibrate a model of residential mobility and school choice. More recent work by Nechyba (2000, 2003) allows variation in additional dimensions, including the quality of housing stock, and adds institutional detail on funding.

26. Thus in both districts, $t_a = t_b = \beta$. The share of income spent on housing is $1 - \alpha - \beta$. Hence the households of type i that populate district j spend in total $(1 - \alpha - \beta)n_i y_i$ to purchase the given quantity H_j of housing. Assuming the rich populate district a and the poor populate district b, the equilibrium housing prices are $p_a = (1 - \alpha - \beta)n_r y_r/H_a$ and $p_b = (1 - \alpha - \beta)n_p y_p/H_b$. The utility of a rich household in district a then equals

$$V_{ra} = \alpha \ln(\alpha y_r) + \beta \ln(\beta y_r) + \gamma \ln(y_r) + (1 - \alpha - \beta) \ln((1 - \alpha - \beta)y_r/p_a),$$

and the utility of a poor household in district b equals

$$V_{pb} = \alpha \ln(\alpha y_p) + \beta \ln(\beta y_p) + \gamma \ln(y_p) + (1 - \alpha - \beta) \ln((1 - \alpha - \beta)y_p/p_b).$$

27. Its utility after moving would be

$$W_{rb} = \alpha \ln(\alpha(1 - \beta)y_r) + \beta \ln(\beta(1 - \beta)y_r) + \gamma \ln(y_r)$$

$$+ (1 - \alpha - \beta) \ln((1 - \alpha - \beta)(1 - \beta)y_r/p_b).$$

For the move to be worthwhile, this must be greater than its utility were it to remain in district a—that is, $W_{rb} - V_{ra} = \ln(1 - \beta) + (1 - \alpha - \beta) \ln(p_a/p_b)$ must be positive. As a separating equilibrium is assumed to hold before the move, equation (7.5) holds, implying that moving is worthwhile if $(\beta + \gamma) \ln(y_r/y_p) > -\ln(1 - \beta)$.

28. An alternative, more direct approach is to estimate the tuition elasticity of private enrollment from microdata on individual schooling decisions. However, this requires controlling for school quality. Regressions of individual schooling decisions on private tuition levels by Long and Toma (1988) and Buddin et al. (1998) failed to identify a significant price effect, but Lankford and Wyckoff (1992) found large significant elasticities: -0.92 for elementary and -3.67 for secondary education.

29. Moreover, as indicated above, savings are likely to materialize more slowly than voucher costs, as the costs of the program are immediate while savings are realized fully only after the public school system gradually adapts to its reduced numbers.

30. This follows a similar calculation by Hoyt and Lee (1998), who conclude on the basis of previous calibrations that an unrestricted voucher of moderate size should generally have a beneficial fiscal effect—assuming that marginal savings per student equal average student cost in public education and that no additional fixed costs are entailed in implementing the voucher system.

31. Tuition in Catholic schools is, on average, less than half of spending per pupil in public schools. Moreover, such schools often make further allowances for the very poor. When the Cleveland voucher program, which was open to religious schools, stipulated that all participating families contribute at least 10 percent of tuition, parochial schools often accepted donations of parents' time as payment in kind (*Zelman et al. v. Simmons-Harris et al.*, 2002).

32. Of course, private nonsectarian schools may also offer reduced tuition to disadvantaged children for a variety of reasons: a sense of public service, the value of a diverse student body, marginal costs that are below average costs. However, the scope for such reductions is more limited, and the motivation may not be as strong as in religious schools.

Chapter 8

1. Socialization and character building were always viewed as primary goals of education. Rousseau (1979/1762) emphasized the role of education in teaching the child to live in harmony with others. Adam Smith (1976/1776, bk. 5, ch. 1, art. 2) analyzed in detail the practical advantages of education for maintaining social order: promoting respect for one's "lawful superiors" and preventing "any wanton or unnecessary opposition to the measures of government." Herbert Spencer (1851, pt. 2, ch. 17, p. 180) plainly wrote, "Education has for its object the formation of character."

2. Relatedly, in Britain universal education came to be viewed as an essential concomitant of the extension of the franchise in the late nineteenth and early twentieth centuries (Dicey, 1962/1914).

3. The formal analysis in this chapter follows Gradstein and Justman (2001, 2002).

4. This holds when the advantages of cooperation increase at a decreasing rate while the probability of effecting a successful transaction, as a function of cultural distance, decreases at an increasing rate.

5. This implicitly assumes that agents have no control over whom they interact with. Bisin and Verdier's (2000, 2001) analysis of socialization through family relationships explicitly assumes that the cost of interaction between any two agents increases with the social distance between the two.

6. The effect of the home environment can easily be incorporated in this formulation.

7. Because the social orientation of the two groups is initially symmetric around $\frac{1}{2}$, the same also applies in all subsequent periods, so that Δ_t fully determines p_{rt} and p_{gt}, we have $p_{rt} = \frac{1}{2} - \frac{1}{2}\Delta_t$ and $p_{gt} = \frac{1}{2} + \frac{1}{2}\Delta_t$, and $|p_{jt} - p_{jt+1}| = \frac{1}{2}(\Delta_t - \Delta_{t+1})$ for $j = r, g$.

8. As education is uniform within each group, we have for $j = r, g$,

$$\Pi_t(p_{jt+1}) = \frac{1}{2}[1 + D(\Delta_{t+1})], \quad \text{and} \quad d\Pi_t(p_{jt+1})/dp_{jt+1} = \frac{1}{2}D'(\Delta_{t+1}).$$

9. The distance to one's own group is 0, where $D(0) = 1$, the distance to the other social group is Δ_{t+1}, and the two groups are the same size.

10. In this light, the decisions of governments to provide socially uniform schooling rather than coordinated sectoral diversity might be viewed as a "second-best" response within these constraints. A related difficulty arises when the central government is too weak to fully control a centralized school system. The modern regulation of schooling by the state was made possible by the emergence of strong central governments supported by innovations in transportation and information technologies.

11. The evolution of public education in nineteenth-century Europe, frequently marked by bitter struggles between church and state, is telling in this regard (Green, 1990).

12. This follows an approach in the literature on legislative bargaining that assumes the ruling coalition gains maximal power and is able to capture the entire surplus even if it commands only a minimal majority (e.g., Riker, 1962; Baron and Ferejohn, 1989).

13. In any event, the centralized solution is not Pareto efficient: it induces overly rapid convergence to complete uniformity and thus imposes an excessive psychic cost on the parent generation.

14. This applies to voluntary migration from Europe and East Asia. Comparing inter-marriage rates of children and grandchildren of immigrants, Jencks (2001, p. 58) esti-mates that "the proportion marrying outside their own ethnic group rose from 43 to 73 percent among Italians, from 53 to 80 percent among Poles, from 74 to 91 percent among Czechs, and from 76 to 92 percent among Hungarians." The image of American society as a melting pot goes back at least to Zangwill (1994/1908).

15. The small experimental voucher programs described in the preceding chapter are the few exceptions.

16. The existence of a clear majority allows us to sidestep the thorny issue of existence of political equilibrium.

17. The assumption here is that the $\{a_{it}\}$ are i.i.d. in each generation, with a skewed dis-tribution such that their mean always exceeds their median, and that the initial distribu-tion of a_{i0} is uncorrelated with the initial income distribution, implying the lack of such correlation in future periods, too. In the interest of simplicity, we ignore here the inter-generational correlation of incomes that is at the center of chapter 5.

18. Because all minority parents initially have the same cultural orientation and the sep-arable form of the utility function implies that school choice is independent of income, they all want the same cultural orientation for their schools and send their children to the same type of school. Hence, along the transition path, the composition of the two popu-lation groups will remain the same as long as the two groups remain distinct, $w_{t+1} = w_t$.

19. Empirical research has repeatedly shown that linguistic assimilation positively affects immigrants' earnings (Chiswick, 1978, 1991).

20. This can be viewed as a simplified version of the model of school choice in chapter 7, above, where a related threshold is derived. See also Gradstein and Justman (2001) for further details.

21. A household with income y_{it} pays $\tau_t y_{it}$ in taxes and receives $\tau_t Y_t / w_{t+1}$ in education spending. The tax price of a dollar of education spending is then $w_{t+1} y_{it} / Y_t$.

22. See, e.g., Rangazas (1995a), Glazer and Niskanen (1997), and Hoyt and Lee (1998).

References

Acemoglu, D. 1996. "A Microfoundation for Social Increasing Returns in Human Capital." *Quarterly Journal of Economics* 111: 779–804.

Acemoglu, D., and J. D. Angrist. 2000. "How Large Are Human Capital Externalities? Evidence from Compulsory Schooling Laws." *NBER Macroeconomics Annual* 15: 9–59.

Acemoglu, D., M. Kremer, and A. Mian. 2003. "Incentives in Markets, Firms and Governments." NBER Working Paper No. 9802. Cambridge, MA.

Acemoglu, D., and J. A. Robinson. 2000. "Why Did the West Extend the Franchise? Democracy, Inequality, and Growth in Historical Perspective." *Quarterly Journal of Economics* 115: 1167–1199.

Acemoglu, D., and J. A. Robinson. 2001. "A Theory of Political Transitions." *American Economic Review* 91: 938–963.

Adelman, I., and C. T. Morris. 1967. *Society, Politics and Economic Development.* Baltimore: Johns Hopkins Press.

Adelman, I., and C. T. Morris. 1973. *Economic Growth and Social Equity in Developing Countries.* Stanford, CA: Stanford University Press.

Ades, A., and T. Verdier. 1996. "The Rise and Fall of Elites: Economic Development and Social Polarization in Rent-Seeking Societies." CEPR Discussion Paper No. 1495. London.

Aghion, P., and P. Bolton. 1997. "A Trickle-Down Theory of Growth and Development with Debt-Overhang." *Review of Economic Studies* 64: 151–172.

Aitchison, J., and J. A. C. Brown. 1969. *The Lognormal Distribution.* London: Cambridge University Press.

Alesina, A., R. Baqir, and W. Easterly. 1999. "Public Goods and Ethnic Divisions." *Quarterly Journal of Economics* 114: 1243–1284.

Alesina, A., and E. La Ferrara. 2000. "Participation in Heterogeneous Communities." *Quarterly Journal of Economics* 115: 847–904.

Alesina, A., and R. Perotti. 1996. "Income Distribution, Political Instability and Investment." *European Economic Review* 40: 1203–1225.

Alesina, A., and D. Rodrik. 1994. "Distributive Politics and Economic Growth." *Quarterly Journal of Economics* 109: 465–490.

Andreoni, J. 1989. "Giving with Impure Altruism: Applications to Charity and Ricardian Equivalence." *Journal of Political Economy* 97: 1447–1458.

Angrist, J. D., and V. Lavy. 1999. "Using Maimonides' Rule to Estimate the Effect of Class Size on Scholastic Achievement." *Quarterly Journal of Economics* 114: 533–575.

Arrow, K. J. 1971. "The Utilitarian Approach to the Concept of Equality in Public Expenditure." *Quarterly Journal of Economics* 85: 409–415.

Arrow, K. J. 1973. "Higher Education as a Filter." *Journal of Public Economics* 2: 193–216.

Ashenfelter, O. C., C. Harmon, and H. Oosterbeek. 1999. "A Review of Estimates of the Schooling/Earnings Relationship, with Tests for Publication Bias." *Labour Economics* 6: 453–470.

Ashenfelter, O. C., and S. Kelley Jr. 1975. "Determinants of Participation in Presidential Elections." *Journal of Law and Economics* 18: 695–733.

Ashenfelter, O. C., and C. E. Rouse. 1998. "Income, Schooling, and Ability: Evidence from a New Sample of Twins." *Quarterly Journal of Economics* 113: 253–284.

Ashenfelter, O. C., and C. E. Rouse. 2000. "Schooling, Intelligence, and Income in America: Cracks in the Bell Curve." In K. J. Arrow, S. Bowles, and S. Durlauf, eds., *Meritocracy and Economic Inequality* (pp. 89–117). Princeton, N.J.: Princeton University Press.

Babs Fafunwa, A., and J. U. Aisiku. 1982. *Education in Africa: A Comparative Analysis.* London: George Allen & Unwin.

Banerjee, A., and A. Newman. 1993. "Occupational Choice and the Process of Development." *Journal of Political Economy* 101: 274–299.

Baron, D. P., and J. A. Ferejohn. 1989. "Bargaining in Legislatures." *American Political Science Review* 83: 1181–1206.

Barro, R. J. 1991. "Economic Growth in a Cross-Section of Countries." *Quarterly Journal of Economics* 106: 407–443.

Barro, R. J. 2001. "Human Capital and Growth." *American Economic Review, Papers and Proceedings* 91: 12–17.

Barro, R. J., and J.-W. Lee. 1993. "International Comparisons of Educational Attainment." *Journal of Monetary Economics* 32: 363–394.

Barro, R. J., and X. Sala-i-Martin. 1995. *Economic Growth.* New York: McGraw-Hill.

Becker, G. S. 1993. *Human Capital: A Theoretical and Empirical Analysis, with Special Reference to Education.* Chicago: University of Chicago Press. Originally published in 1964.

Becker, G. S., and B. R. Chiswick. 1966. "Education and the Distribution of Earnings." *American Economic Review* 56: 358–369.

Becker, G. S., K. Murphy, and R. Tamura. 1990. "Human Capital, Fertility, and Economic Growth." *Journal of Political Economy* 98: S12–S37.

Becker, G. S., and N. Tomes. 1979. "An Equilibrium Theory of the Distribution of Income and Intergenerational Mobility." *Journal of Political Economy* 87: 1153–1189.

Becker, G. S., and N. Tomes. 1986. "Human Capital and the Rise and Fall of Families." *Journal of Labor Economics* 4: S1–S39.

Behrman, J., and M. R. Rosenzweig. 1999. "'Ability' Biases in Schooling Returns and Twins: A Test and New Estimates." *Economics of Education Review* 18: 159–167.

Behrman, J., and P. Taubman. 1985. "Intergenerational Earnings and Mobility in the United States: Some Estimates and a Test of Becker's Intergenerational Endowments Model." *Review of Economics and Statistics* 67: 144–151.

Belfield, C. R., and H. M. Levin. 2002. "The Effects of Competition between Schools on Educational Outcomes" *Review of Educational Research* 72: 279–341.

Bénabou, R. 1993. "Workings of a City: Location, Education, and Production." *Quarterly Journal of Economics* 108: 619–652.

Bénabou, R. 1994. "Human Capital, Inequality, and Growth: A Local Perspective." *European Economic Review* 38: 817–826.

Bénabou, R. 1996a. "Equity and Efficiency in Human Capital Investment: The Local Connection." *Review of Economic Studies* 63: 237–264.

Bénabou, R. 1996b. "Heterogeneity, Stratification, and Growth: Macroeconomic Implications of Community Structure and School Finance." *American Economic Review* 86: 584–609.

Bénabou, R. 1996c. "Inequality and Growth." *NBER Macroeconomics Annual* 11: 11–74.

Bénabou, R. 2000. "Unequal Societies: Income Distribution and the Social Contract." *American Economic Review* 90: 96–129.

Benhabib, J., and A. Rustichini. 1996. "Social Conflict and Growth." *Journal of Economic Growth* 1: 125–142.

Benhabib, J., and M. Spiegel. 1994. "The Role of Human Capital in Economic Development: Evidence from Aggregate Cross-Country Data." *Journal of Monetary Economics* 34: 143–174.

Bergstrom, T., D. Rubinfeld, and P. Shapiro. 1982. "Micro-Based Estimates of Demand Functions for Local School Expenditures." *Econometrica* 50: 1183–1205.

Bertocchi, G., and M. Spagat. 2004. "The Evolution of Modern Educational Systems: Technical vs. General Education, Distributional Conflict, and Growth." *Journal of Development Economics* 73: 559–582.

Besley, T., and S. Coate. 1998. "Centralized versus Decentralized Provision of Local Public Goods: A Political Economy Approach." National Bureau of Economic Research Working Paper No. 7084. Cambridge, MA.

Betts, J. R. 1996. "Is there a Link between School Inputs and Earnings? Fresh Scrunity of an Old Literature." Discussion Paper No. 96:09, Department of Economics, University of California.

Bils, M., and P. J. Klenow. 2000. "Does Schooling Cause Growth?" *American Economic Review* 90: 1160–1183.

Bisin, A., and T. Verdier. 2000. "'Beyond the Melting Pot': Cultural Transmission, Marriage, and the Evolution of Ethnic and Religious Traits." *Quarterly Journal of Economics* 115: 955–988.

Bisin, A., and T. Verdier. 2001. "The Economics of Cultural Transmission and the Dynamics of Preferences." *Journal of Economic Theory* 97: 298–319.

Black, D. 1948. "On the Rationale of Group Decision Making." *Journal of Political Economy* 56: 23–34.

Boadway, R., N. Marceau, and M. Marchand. 1996. "Investment in Education and the Time Inconsistency of Redistributive Tax Policy." *Economica* 63: 171–189.

Bourguignon, F. 1981. "Pareto-Superiority of Unegalitarian Equilibria in Stiglitz' Model of Wealth Distribution with Convex Savings Function." *Econometrica* 49: 1469–1475.

Bourguignon, F., and T. Verdier. 2000. "Oligarchy, Democracy, Inequality and Growth." *Journal of Development Economics* 62: 285–313.

Bovenberg, L. A., and B. Jacobs. 2001. "Redistribution and Education Subsidies Are Siamese Twins." CEPR Discussion Paper No. 3099. London.

Bowles, S., and H. Gintis. 1976. *Schooling in Capitalist America: Educational Reform and the Contradictions of Economic Life*. New York: Basic Books.

Brady, H., S. Verba, and K. L. Schlozman. 1995. "Beyond SES: A Resource Model of Political Participation." *American Political Science Review* 89: 271–294.

Brown v. Board of Education, 347 U.S. 483 (1954).

Bruce, N., and M. Waldman. 1991. "Transfers in Kind: Why They Can Be Efficient and Nonpaternalistic." *American Economic Review* 81: 1345–1351.

Brunner, E., and J. Sonstelie. 2003. "Homeowners, Property Values, and the Political Economy of the School Voucher." *Journal of Urban Economics* 54: 239–257.

Bruno, M. 1976. "Equality, Complementarity and the Incidence of Public Expenditure." *Journal of Public Economics* 6: 395–407.

Buddin, R., J. Cordes, and S. N. Kirby. 1998. "School Choice in California: Who Chooses Private Schools?" *Journal of Urban Economics* 44: 110–134.

Cameron, S., and J. J. Heckman. 2001. "The Dynamics of Educational Attainment for Black, Hispanic, and White Males." *Journal of Political Economy* 109: 455–499.

Card, D. 1995. "Earnings, Schooling, and Ability Revisited." *Research in Labor Economics* 14: 23–48.

Card, D., and A. B. Krueger. 1992. "Does School Quality Matter? Returns to Education and the Characteristics of Public Schools in the United States." *Journal of Political Economy* 100: 1–40.

Card, D., and A. B. Krueger. 1996. "School Resources and Student Outcomes: An Overview of the Literature and New Evidence from North and South Carolina." *Journal of Economic Perspectives* 10(4): 31–50.

Card, D., and A. A. Payne. 2002. "School Finance Reform, the Distribution of School Spending, and the Distribution of Student Test Scores." *Journal of Public Economics* 83: 49–82.

Carneiro, P., J. J. Heckman, and D. Manoli. 2003. "Human Capital Policy." In J. J. Heckman and A. Krueger, eds., *Inequality in America: What Role for Human Capital Policies?* Cambridge, MA: MIT Press.

Checchi, D. 1997. "Education and Intergenerational Mobility in Occupations: A Comparative Study." *American Journal of Economics and Sociology* 56: 331–352.

Checchi, D., A. Ichino, and A. Rustichini. 1999. "More Equal but Less Mobile? Education Financing and Intergenerational Mobility in Italy and in the US." *Journal of Public Economics* 74: 351–393.

Chenery, H. B., M. S. Ahluwalia, C. Bell, J. H. Dulloy, and R. Jolly. 1974. *Redistribution with Growth*. New York: Oxford University Press.

Chenery, H. B., and M. Syrquin. 1975. *Patterns of Development, 1950–1970*. London: Oxford University Press for the World Bank.

Chiswick, B. R. 1978. "The Effect of Americanization on Earnings of Foreign-Born Men." *Journal of Political Economy* 86: 897–921.

Chiswick, B. R. 1991. "Speaking, Reading, and Earnings among Low-Skilled Immigrants." *Journal of Labor Economics* 9: 149–170.

Chubb, J. E., and T. M. Moe. 1990. *Politics, Markets, and America's Schools*. Washington, DC: Brookings Institution.

Clotfelter, C. 1976. "School Desegregation, 'Tipping' and Private School Enrollment." *Journal of Human Resources* 11: 28–50.

Cohen, D., and M. Soto. 2001. "Growth and Human Capital: Good Data, Good Results." CEPR Discussion Paper No. 3025. London.

Cohen-Zada, D. 2002. "Preserving Religious Values through Education: Economic Analysis and Evidence from the US." Working Paper, Ben-Gurion University.

Cohen-Zada, D., and M. Justman. 2002. "The Religious Factor in Private Education." Working Paper, Ben Gurion University.

Cohen-Zada, D., and M. Justman. 2003. "The Political Economy of School Choice: Linking Theory and Evidence." *Journal of Urban Economics* 54: 277–308.

Coleman, J. S. 1988. "Social Capital in the Creation of Human Capital." *American Journal of Sociology* 94: S95–S120.

Cox, C., and Lemaitre, M. J. 1999. "Market and State Principles of Reform in Chilean Education: Policies and Results." In G. Perry and D. M. Leipziger, eds., *Chile: Recent Policy Lessons and Emerging Challenges* (pp. 159–188). Washington, DC: World Bank.

Cubberley, E. 1919. *Public Education in the United States*. Boston: Houghton Mifflin.

De Gregorio, J., and S. J. Kim. 2000. "Credit Markets with Differences in Abilities: Education, Distribution and Growth." *International Economic Review* 41: 579–607.

De Gregorio, J., and J.-W. Lee. 2002. "Education and Income Distribution: New Evidence from Cross-Country Data." *Review of Income and Wealth* 48: 395–416.

De la Fuente, A., and R. Domenech. 2000. "Human Capital in Growth Regressions: How Much Difference Does Data Quality Make?" CEPR Discussion Paper No. 2466. London.

Dicey, A. V. 1962. *Lectures on the Relation between Law and Public Opinion in England during the Nineteenth Century*. 2nd ed. London: Macmillan. Originally published in 1914.

DiPasquale, D., and E. L. Glaeser. 1998. "The Los Angeles Riot and the Economics of Urban Unrest." *Journal of Urban Economics* 43: 52–78.

Downes, T., and D. Figlio. 1999. "Economic Inequality and the Provision of Schooling." *Federal Reserve Bank of New York Economic Policy Review* 5: 99–110.

Durkheim, E. 1956. *Education and Sociology.* Trans. by S. D. Fox. Free Press: Glencoe, IL. Originally published in 1922.

Easterly, W., and R. Levine. 1997. "Africa's Growth Tragedy: Policies and Ethnic Divisions." *Quarterly Journal of Economics* 112: 1203–1250.

Easterly, W., and S. Rebelo. 1993. "Fiscal Policy and Growth: An Empirical Investigation." *Journal of Monetary Economics* 32: 417–458.

Eckstein, Z., and I. Zilcha. 1994. "The Effects of Compulsory Schooling on Growth, Income Distribution and Welfare." *Journal of Public Economics* 54: 339–359.

Edin, P.-A., P. Fredriksson, and O. Aaslund. 2003. "Ethnic Enclaves and the Economic Success of Immigrants: Evidence from a Natural Experiment." *Quarterly Journal of Economics* 118: 329–357.

Edwards, N., and H. G. Richey. 1963. *The School in the American Social Order.* Boston: Houghton Mifflin.

Ehrlich, I. 1975. "On the Relation between Education and Crime." In F. T. Juster, ed., *Education, Income, and Human Behavior* (pp. 313–338). New York: McGraw-Hill.

Epple, D., R. Filimon, and T. Romer. 1984. "Equilibrium among Local Jurisdictions: Toward an Integrated Treatment of Voting and Residential Choice." *Journal of Public Economics* 24: 281–308.

Epple, D., and R. Romano. 1996a. "Ends against the Middle: Determining Public Service Provision When There Are Private Alternatives." *Journal of Public Economics* 62: 297–325.

Epple, D., and R. Romano. 1996b. "Public Provision of Private Goods." *Journal of Political Economy* 104: 57–84.

Epple, D., and R. Romano. 1998. "Competition between Private and Public Schools, Vouchers and Peer-Group Effects." *American Economic Review* 88: 33–62.

Epple, D., and T. Romer. 1991. "Mobility and Redistribution." *Journal of Political Economy* 99: 828–858.

Epple, D., and H. Sieg. 1999. "Estimating Equilibrium Models of Local Jurisdictions." *Journal of Political Economy* 107: 645–682.

Erikson, R., and J. H. Goldthorpe. 1993. *The Constant Flux: A Study of Class Mobility in Industrial Societies.* New York: Oxford University Press.

European Commission. 1995. *Structures of the Education and Initial Training Systems in the European Union.* 2nd ed. Luxembourg: European Commission.

Evans, W., and R. Schwab. 1995. "Finishing High School and Starting College: Do Catholic Schools Make a Difference?" *Quarterly Journal of Economics* 110: 947–974.

Fernandez, R., and R. Rogerson. 1996. "Income Distribution, Communities, and the Quality of Public Education." *Quarterly Journal of Economics* 111: 135–164.

Fernandez, R., and R. Rogerson. 1998. "Public Education and Income Distribution: A Dynamic Quantitative Evaluation of Education-Finance Reform." *American Economic Review* 88: 813–833.

Fernandez, R., and R. Rogerson. 1999. "Education Finance Reform and Investment in Human Capital: Lessons from California." *Journal of Public Economics* 74: 327–350.

Fernandez, R., and R. Rogerson. 2001. "The Determinants of Public Education Expenditures: Longer-Run Evidence from the States." *Journal of Education Finance* 27: 567–583.

Fernandez, R., and R. Rogerson. 2003. "Equity and Resources: An Analysis of Education Finance Systems." *Journal of Political Economy* 111: 858–897.

Filer, J. E., L. W. Kenny, and R. B. Morton. 1991. "Voting Laws, Educational Politics and Minority Turnout." *Journal of Law and Economics* 34: 371–393.

Finer, S. E. 1997. *The History of Government from the Earliest Times.* Oxford: Oxford University Press.

Finn Jr., C. E., B. V. Manno, and G. Vanourek. 2000. *Charter Schools in Action: Renewing Public Education.* Princeton, NJ: Princeton University Press.

Fischel, W. A. 2002. "An Economic Case against Vouchers: Why Local Public Schools Are a Local Public Good." Dartmouth College Working Paper 02-01. Hanover, NH.

Fiske, E., and H. Ladd. 2000. *When Schools Compete.* Washington, DC: Brookings Institution.

Flug, K., A. Spilimbergo, and E. Wachtenheim. 1998. "Investment in Education: Do Economic Volatility and Credit Constraints Matter?" *Journal of Development Economics* 55: 465–481.

Friedman, M. 1962. *Capitalism and Freedom.* Chicago: University of Chicago Press.

Fukuyama, F. 1995. *Trust: The Social Virtues and the Creation of Prosperity.* New York: Free Press.

Galor, O., and O. Moav. 2001. "Das Human Kapital." CEPR Discussion Paper No. 2701. London.

Galor, O., and J. Zeira. 1993. "Income Distribution and Macroeconomics." *Review of Economic Studies* 60: 35–52.

Gans, J. S., and M. Smart. 1996. "Majority Voting with Single-Crossing Preferences." *Journal of Public Economics* 59: 219–237.

Gauri, V. 1998. *School Choice in Chile: Two Decades of Educational Reform.* Pittsburgh: University of Pittsburgh Press.

Gilboa, Y. 2003. "Kibbutz Education: Implications for Helping Children from Disadvantaged Backgrounds." *Economic Quarterly* 50: 572–602.

Glaeser, E. L., J. A. Scheinkman, and A. Shleifer. 1995. "Economic Growth in a Cross-Section of Cities." *Journal of Monetary Economics* 36: 117–143.

Glazer, A., and E. Niskanen. 1997. "Why Voters May Prefer Congested Public Clubs." *Journal of Public Economics* 65: 37–44.

Glomm, G., and B. Ravikumar. 1992. "Public versus Private Investment in Human Capital: Endogenous Growth and Income Inequality." *Journal of Political Economy* 100: 818–834.

Glomm, G., and B. Ravikumar. 1998. "Opting out of Publicly Provided Services: A Majority Voting Result." *Social Choice and Welfare* 15: 187–199.

Goldin, C. 1998. "America's Graduation from High School: The Evolution and Spread of Secondary Schooling in the Twentieth Century." *Journal of Economic History* 58: 345–374.

Goldin, C. 1999. "A Brief History of Education in the United States." NBER Working Paper, Historical Paper No. 119. Cambridge, MA.

Goldin, C., and L. F. Katz. 1999. "Human Capital and Social Capital: The Rise of Secondary Schooling in America, 1910 to 1940." *Journal of Interdisciplinary History* 26 (Spring): 683–723.

Good, H. G., and J. D. Teller. 1969. *A History of Western Education*. 3rd ed. London: Macmillan.

Gouveia, M. R. 1997. "Majority Rule and Public Provision of a Private Good." *Public Choice* 93: 221–244.

Gradstein, M. 2000. "An Economic Rationale for Public Education: The Value of Commitment." *Journal of Monetary Economics*, 45: 463–474.

Gradstein, M., and M. Justman. 1996. "The Political Economy of Mixed Public and Private Schooling: A Dynamic Analysis." *International Tax and Public Finance* 3: 297–310.

Gradstein, M., and M. Justman. 1997. "Democratic Choice of an Education Regime: Implications for Growth and Income Distribution." *Journal of Economic Growth* 2: 169–183.

Gradstein, M., and M. Justman. 2000. "Human Capital, Social Capital, and Public Schooling." *European Economic Review* 44: 879–890.

Gradstein, M., and M. Justman. 2001. "Public Education and the Melting Pot." CEPR Discussion Paper No. 2924. London.

Gradstein, M., and M. Justman. 2002. "Education, Social Cohesion, and Economic Growth." *American Economic Review* 92: 1192–1204.

Green, A. 1990. *Education and State Formation*. New York: St. Martin's Press.

Greif, A. 1993. "Contract Enforceability and Economic Institutions in Early Trade: The Maghribi Traders' Coalition." *American Economic Review* 83: 525–548.

Griliches, Z. 1997. "Education, Human Capital, and Growth: A Personal Perspective." *Journal of Labor Economics* 15: S330–S344.

Grossman, H. I. 1991. "A General Equilibrium Model of Insurrections." *American Economic Review* 81: 912–921.

Grossman, H. I. 1994. "Production, Appropriation, and Land Reform." *American Economic Review* 84: 705–712.

Gundlach, E., L. Woessmann, and J. Gmelin. 2001. "The Decline of Schooling Productivity in OECD Countries." *Economic Journal* 111: 135–147.

Hanushek, E. A. 1986. "The Economics of Schooling: Production and Efficiency in Public Schools." *Journal of Economic Literature* 24: 1141–1177.

Hanushek, E. A. 2003. "The Failure of Input-Based Schooling Policies." *Economic Journal* 113: F64–F98.

Hanushek, E. A., and D. D. Kimko. 2000. "Schooling, Labor Force Quality, and the Growth of Nations." *American Economic Review* 90: 1184–1208.

Hassel, B. C. 1998. "Charter Schools: Politics and Practice in Four States." In P. E. Peterson and B. C. Hassel, eds., *Learning from School Choice* (pp. 249–271). Washington, DC: Brookings Institution.

Hassler, J., and J. V. R. Mora. 2000. "Intelligence, Social Mobility, and Growth." *American Economic Review* 90: 888–908.

Haveman, R. H., and B. L. Wolfe. 1984. "Schooling and Economic Well-Being: The Role of Nonmarket Effects." *Journal of Human Resources* 19: 377–407.

Heckman, J. J. 1995. "Lessons from the Bell Curve." *Journal of Political Economy* 103: 1091–1120.

Heckman, J. J. 2000. "Policies to Foster Human Capital." *Research in Economics* 54: 3–56.

Herrnstein, R., and C. Murray. 1994. *The Bell Curve: Intelligence and Class Structure in American Life*. New York: Free Press.

Heston, A., and Summers, R. 1991. "The Penn World Table (Mark 5): An Expanded Set of International Comparisons, 1950–1988." *Quarterly Journal of Economics* 106: 327–368.

Hines Jr., J. R., and R. H. Thaler. 1995. "The Flypaper Effect." *Journal of Economic Perspectives* 9: 217–226.

Hoxby, C. M. 1998. "What Do America's 'Traditional' Forms of School Choice Teach Us about School Choice Reforms?" *Federal Reserve Bank of New York Economic Policy Review* 4: 47–59.

Howell, W. G., P. E. Peterson, P. J. Wolf, and D. E. Campbell. 2002. *The Education Gap*. Washington, DC: Brookings Institution.

Hoyt, W., and K. Lee. 1998. "Educational Vouchers, Welfare Effects and Voting." *Journal of Public Economics* 69: 211–228.

Hsieh, C.-T., and M. Urquiola. 2003. "When Schools Compete, How Do They Compete? An Assessment of Chile's Nationwide School Voucher Program." NBER Working Paper No. 10008. Cambridge, MA.

Hume, D. 1742. *Essays, Moral and Political*. Edinburgh: A. Kincaid.

Husted, T. A., and L. W. Kenny. 1997. "The Effect of the Expansion of the Voting Franchise on the Size of Government." *Journal of Political Economy* 105: 54–82.

James, E. 1987. "The Public-Private Division of Responsibility for Education: An International Comparison." *Economics of Education Review* 6: 1–14.

James, E. 1993. "Why Do Different Countries Choose a Different Public-Private Mix of Educational Services?" *Journal of Human Resources* 28: 572–592.

Jencks, C. 2001. "Who Should Get In?" *New York Review of Books* 29 November: 57–63 (pt. 1) and 20 December: 94–102 (pt. 2).

Justman, M., and M. Gradstein. 1999. "Industrial Revolution, Political Transition and the Subsequent Decline in Inequality in Nineteenth-Century Britain." *Explorations in Economic History* 36: 109–127.

Katz, M. B. 1976. "The Origins of Public Education: A Reassessment" *History of Education Quarterly* 16: 381–407.

Knack, S., and P. Keefer. 1997. "Does Social Capital Have an Economic Payoff? A Cross-Country Investigation." *Quarterly Journal of Economics* 112: 207–227.

Kotkin, J. 1992. *Tribes: How Race, Religion, and Identity Determine Success in the New Global Economy.* New York: Random House.

Kremer, M. 1997. "How Much Does Sorting Increase Inequality?" *Quarterly Journal of Economics* 112: 115–140.

Kremer, M., and A. Sarychev. 1998. "Why Do Governments Operate Schools?" Mimeo, Harvard University.

Krueger, A. B. 1999. "Experimental Estimates of Education Production Functions." *Quarterly Journal of Economics* 114: 497–532.

Krueger, A. B., and M. Lindahl. 2001. "Education for Growth: Why and for Whom?" *Journal of Economic Literature* 39: 1101–1136.

Kuznets, S. 1966. *Modern Economic Growth.* New Haven, CT: Yale University Press.

Ladd, H. 2002. "School Vouchers: A Critical View" *Journal of Economic Perspectives* 16(4): 3–24.

Lamberti, M. 1989. *State, Society, and the Elementary School in Imperial Germany.* New York: Oxford University Press.

Lane, P., and A. Tornell. 1996. "Power, Growth and the Voracity Effect." *Journal of Economic Growth* 1: 213–241.

Lankford, H., and J. Wyckoff. 1992. "Primary and Secondary School Choice among Public and Religious Alternatives." *Economics of Education Review* 4: 317–337.

La Porta, R., F. Lopez-de-Silanes, A. Shleifer, and R. W. Vishny. 1997. "Trust in Large Organizations." *American Economic Review, Papers and Proceedings* 87: 333–338.

LaRocque, N. 1999. "The Regulatory Framework for the New Zealand School Sector: A Description." Manuscript. Washington, DC: World Bank.

Lazear, E. P. 1999. "Culture and Language." *Journal of Political Economy* 107: S95–S126.

Levin, H., and C. Driver. 1997. "Costs of an Educational Voucher System." *Educational Economics* 5: 265–283.

Lindert, P. H. 1994. "The Rise of Social Spending: 1880–1930." *Explorations in Economic History* 31: 1–37.

Lindert, P. H., and J. G. Williamson. 1985. "Growth, Equality and History." *Explorations in Economic History* 22: 341–377.

Lochner, L., and E. Moretti. 2001. "The Effect of Education on Crime: Evidence from Prison Inmates, Arrests, and Self-Reports." NBER Working Paper No. 8605. Cambridge, MA.

Long, J., and E. Toma. 1988. "The Determinants of Private School Attendance, 1970–1980." *Review of Economics and Statistics* 70: 351–356.

Lott, J. R. 1990. "An Explanation for Public Provision of Schooling: The Importance of Indoctrination." *Journal of Law and Economics* 33: 199–231.

Lott, J. R. 1999. "Public Schooling, Indoctrination, and Totalitarianism." *Journal of Political Economy* 107: 127–157.

Loury, G. 1981. "Intergenerational Transfers and the Distribution of Earnings." *Econometrica* 49: 843–867.

Lucas Jr., R. E. 1988. "On the Mechanics of Economic Development." *Journal of Monetary Economics* 22: 3–42.

Lundgreen, P. 1980. *Sozialgeschichte der deutsche Schule im Überblick.* Göttingen: Vandenhoeck & Ruprecht.

Maddison, A. 1991. *Dynamic Forces in Capitalist Development.* Oxford: Oxford University Press.

Mankiw, G. N., D. Romer, and D. N. Weil. 1992. "A Contribution to the Empirics of Economic Growth." *Quarterly Journal of Economics* 107: 407–437.

Maoz, Y., and O. Moav. 1999. "Intergenerational Mobility and the Process of Development." *Economic Journal* 109: 677–697.

Mauro, P. 1995. "Corruption and Growth." *Quarterly Journal of Economics* 110: 681–712.

Meltzer, A., and S. Richard. 1981. "A Rational Theory of the Size of Government." *Journal of Political Economy* 89: 914–927.

Metz, M. H. 1990. "Potentialities and Problems of Choice in Desegregation Plans." In *Choice and Control in American Education*, Vol. 2, W. H. Clune and J. F. Witte, eds., *The Practice of Choice, Decentralization and School Restructuring* (pp. 111–117). Bristol, PA: Falmer Press.

Miguel, E. 2003. "Tribe or Nation? Nation-Building and Public Goods in Kenya versus Tanzania." Manuscript. University of California, Berkeley, CA.

Miguel, E., and M. K. Gugerty. 2002. "Ethnic Diversity, Social Sanctions, and Public Goods in Kenya." Manuscript. University of California, Berkeley, CA.

Mill, J. S. 1848. *Principles of Political Economy.* New York: Penguin Books, 1970.

Mincer, J. 1974. *Schooling, Earnings, and Experience.* New York: Columbia University Press.

Mocan, H. N., B. Scafidi, and E. Tekin. 2002. "Catholic Schools and Bad Behavior." NBER Working Paper No. 9172. Cambridge, MA.

Moretti, E. 2002. "Estimating the Social Return to Higher Education: Evidence from Longitudinal and Repeated Cross-Sectional Data." NBER Working Paper No. 9108. Cambridge, MA.

Mueller, D. 1989. *Public Choice II.* Cambridge: Cambridge University Press.

Murray, S., W. Evans, and R. Schwab. 1998. "Education Finance Reform and the Distribution of Education Resources." *American Economic Review* 88: 789–812.

National Catholic Educational Association. 1990. *United States Catholic Elementary and Secondary Schools 1989–90.* Washington, DC: NCEA.

National Center for Education Statistics. Various years. *Digest of Education Statistics.* Washington, DC. ⟨http://nces.ed.gov⟩.

Neal, D. 1997. "The Effects of Catholic Secondary Schooling on Educational Attainment." *Journal of Labor Economics* 15: 98–123.

Neal, D. 2002. "How Vouchers Could Change the Market for Education." *Journal of Economic Perspectives* 16(4): 25–44.

Neal, D., and S. Rosen. 2000. "Theories of the Distribution of Earnings." In A. B. Atkinson and F. Bourguignon, eds., *Handbook of Income Distribution* (Vol. 1, pp. 379–427). Amsterdam: Elsevier North-Holland.

Nechyba, T. J. 2000. "Mobility, Targeting, and Private School Vouchers." *American Economic Review* 90: 130–146.

Nechyba, T. J. 2003. "Centralization, Fiscal Federalism and Private School Attendance." *International Economic Review* 44: 179–204.

New State Ice Co. v. Liebmann, 285 U.S. 262 (1932). ⟨http://laws.findlaw.com/us/285/262.html⟩.

OECD. 1998. *Education at a Glance: OECD Indicators*. Paris: OECD.

OECD. 2000. *Investing in Education: Analysis of the 1999 World Education Indicators*. Paris: OECD.

OECD. 2001a. *Education at a Glance: OECD Indicators*. Paris: OECD.

OECD. 2001b. *Knowledge and Skills for Life: First Results from PISA 2000*. Paris: OECD.

OECD. 2002. *Education at a Glance: OECD Indicators*. Paris: OECD.

OECD. 2003. *Literacy Skills for the World of Tomorrow: Further Results from PISA 2000*. Paris: OECD.

Owen, A., and D. N. Weil. 1998. "Intergenerational Earnings Mobility, Inequality, and Growth." *Journal of Monetary Economics* 41: 71–104.

Paine, T. 1984. *The Rights of Man*. London: Penguin Books. Originally published in 1792.

Parry, T. R. 1997a. "Achieving Balance in Decentralization: A Case Study of Education Decentralization in Chile." *World Development* 25: 211–225.

Parry, T. R. 1997b. "Decentralization and Privatization: Education Policy in Chile." *Journal of Public Policy* 17: 107–133.

Perotti, R. 1993. "Political Equilibrium, Income Distribution, and Growth." *Review of Economic Studies* 60: 755–776.

Perotti, R. 1996. "Growth, Income Distribution, and Democracy: What the Data Say." *Journal of Economic Growth* 1: 149–187.

Persson, T., and G. Tabellini. 1994. "Is Inequality Harmful for Growth?" *American Economic Review* 84: 600–621.

Persson, T., and G. Tabellini. 2000. *Political Economics: Explaining Economic Policy*. Cambridge, MA: MIT Press.

Piketty, T. 1997. "The Dynamics of the Wealth Distribution and the Interest Rate with Credit-Rationing." *Review of Economic Studies* 64: 173–189.

Plato. 1901. *The Republic*. Trans. by B. Jowett. New York: Collier, Colonial Press. Originally written in 360 B.C.

Poterba, J. M. 1997. "Demographic Structure and the Political Economy of Public Education." *Journal of Policy Analysis and Management* 16(1): 48–66.

Pritchett, L. 2001. "Where Has All the Education Gone?" *World Bank Economic Review* 15: 367–391.

Pritchett, L. 2003. "'When Will They Ever Learn'? Why All Governments Produce Schooling." BREAD Working Paper No. 31, Harvard University.

Psacharopoulos, G. 1981. "Returns to Education: An Updated International Comparison." *Comparative Education* 17: 321–341.

Psacharopoulos, G. 1994. "Returns to Investment in Education: A Global Update." *World Development* 22: 1325–1343.

Putnam, R. D. 1993. *Making Democracy Work: Civic Traditions in Modern Italy.* Princeton, NJ: Princeton University Press.

Ram, R. 1984. "Population Increase, Economic Growth, Educational Inequality, and Income Distribution: Some Recent Evidence." *Journal of Development Economics* 14: 419–428.

Ram, R. 1987. "Can Educational Expansion Reduce Income Inequality in Less-Developed Countries?" *Economics of Education Review* 8: 185–189.

Rangazas, P. C. 1995a. "Vouchers and Voting: An Initial Estimate Based on the Median Voter Model." *Public Choice* 82: 261–279.

Rangazas, P. C. 1995b. "Vouchers in a Community Choice Model with Zoning." *Quarterly Review of Economics and Finance* 35: 15–39.

Rauch, J. E. 1993. "Productivity Gains from Geographic Concentration of Human Capital: Evidence from the Cities." *Journal of Urban Economics* 34: 380–400.

Riker, W. H. 1962. *The Theory of Political Coalitions.* New Haven, CT: Yale University Press.

Roberts, K. 1977. "Voting over Income Tax Schedules." *Journal of Public Economics* 8: 329–340.

Robinson v. Cahill, 62 N.J. 473, 303 A.2d 273 (1973).

Romer, P. M. 1986. "Increasing Returns and Long-Run Growth." *Journal of Political Economy* 94: 1002–1037.

Romer, T., and H. Rosenthal. 1978. "Political Resource Allocation, Controlled Agendas, and the Status Quo." *Public Choice* 33: 27–43.

Romer, T., H. Rosenthal, and V. Munley. 1992. "Economic Incentives and Political Institutions: Spending and Voting in School Budget Referenda." *Journal of Public Economics* 49: 1–33.

Rousseau, J.-J. 1979. *Emile, or On Education.* Trans. by A. Bloom. New York: Basic Books. Originally published in Paris in 1762.

Rubinfeld, D., and P. Shapiro. 1989. "Micro-Estimation of the Demand for Schooling." *Regional Science and Urban Economics* 19: 381–398.

Rubinfeld, D., P. Shapiro, and J. Roberts. 1987. "Tiebout Bias and the Demand for Local Public Schooling." *Review of Economics and Statistics* 69: 426–437.

Rustichini, A., and J. A. Schmitz. 1991. "Research and Imitation in Long-Run Growth." *Journal of Monetary Economics* 27: 271–292.

Saint-Paul, G., and T. Verdier. 1993. "Education, Democracy and Growth." *Journal of Development Economics* 42: 399–407.

Sander, W. 1997. "Catholic High Schools and Rural Academic Achievement." *American Journal of Agricultural Economics* 79: 1–12.

Schultz, T. W. 1963. *The Economic Value of Education*. New York: Columbia University Press.

Schultz, T. W. 1971. *Investment in Human Capital*. New York: Free Press.

Serrano v. Priest, 5 Cal.3d 584, 487 P.2d 1241 (1971).

Silva, F., and J. Sonstelie. 1995. "Did *Serrano* Cause a Decline in School Spending?" *National Tax Journal* 48: 199–215.

Smith, A. 1976. *An Inquiry into the Nature and Causes of the Wealth of Nations*. Chicago: University of Chicago Press. Originally published in 1776.

Solon, G. 1992. "Intergenerational Mobility in the United States." *American Economic Review* 82: 393–408.

Solow, R. M. 1957. "Technical Change and the Aggregate Production Function." *Review of Economics and Statistics* 39: 312–320.

Sonstelie, J. 1982. "The Welfare Cost of Free Public Schools." *Journal of Political Economy* 90: 794–808.

Spence, A. M. 1973. "Job Market Signaling." *Quarterly Journal of Economics* 87: 355–374.

Spence, A. M. 1975. "Monopoly, Quality, and Regulation." *Bell Journal of Economics* 6: 417–429.

Spencer, H. 1851. *Social Statics*. London: Chapman.

Statistisches Bundesamt. 2000. *Fachserie 11 Bildung und Kultur, Reihe S. 2, Allgemeinbildende und berufliche Schulen 1950 bis 1999*. Stuttgart: Metzler-Poeschel.

Stigler, G. 1970. "Director's Law of Public Income Redistribution." *Journal of Law and Economics* 13: 1–10.

Stiglitz, J. E. 1969. "Distribution of Income and Wealth among Individuals." *Econometrica* 37: 382–397.

Stiglitz, J. E. 1974. "The Demand for Education in Public and Private School Systems." *Journal of Public Economics* 3: 349–385.

Stiglitz, J. E. 1975. "The Theory of Screening, Education, and the Distribution of Income." *American Economic Review* 65: 283–300.

Svensson, J. 1998. "Investment, Property Rights, and Political Instability: Theory and Evidence." *European Economic Review* 42: 1317–1341.

Sylwester, K. 2000. "Income Inequality, Education Expenditures, and Growth." *Journal of Development Economics* 63: 379–398.

Tavares, J., and R. Wacziarg. 2001. "How Democracy Affects Growth." *European Economic Review* 45: 1341–1378.

Temple, J., and P. A. Johnson. 1998. "Social Capability and Economic Growth." *Quarterly Journal of Economics* 113: 965–990.

Teulings, C. N., and T. van Rens. 2003. "Education, Growth and Income Inequality." CEPR Discussion Paper No. 3863. London.

Tiebout, C. 1956. "A Pure Theory of Local Expenditures." *Journal of Political Economy* 64: 416–424.

Tobin, J. 1970. "On Limiting the Domain of Inequality." *Journal of Law and Economics* 13: 263–277.

Topel, R. 1999. "Labor Markets and Economic Growth." In O. C. Ashenfelter and D. Card, eds., *Handbook of Labor Economics* (Vol. 3C, pp. 2943–2984). Amsterdam: North-Holland.

Tornell, A. 1997. "Economic Growth and Decline with Endogenous Property Rights." *Journal of Economic Growth* 2: 219–250.

Tornell, A. 1999. "The Voracity Effect." *American Economic Review* 89: 22–46.

Ulph, D. 1977. "On the Optimal Distribution of Income and Educational Expenditure." *Journal of Public Economics* 8: 341–356.

Usher, D. 1977. "The Welfare Economics of Socialization of Commodities." *Journal of Public Economics* 8: 151–168.

Verba, S., N. Nie, and Kim, J. 1978. *Participation and Political Equality*. Chicago: University of Chicago Press.

Willis, R. J., and S. Rosen. 1979. "Education and Self-Selection." *Journal of Political Economy* 87: S7–S36.

Woessmann, L. 2003. "Schooling Resources, Educational Institutions and Student Performance: the International Evidence." *Oxford Bulletin of Economics and Statistics* 65: 117–170.

Wolfe, B., and S. Zuvekas. 1997. "Non-Market Effects of Education." *International Journal of Education Research* 27: 491–501.

Wyckoff, J. H. 1992. "The Intrastate Equality of Public Primary and Secondary Education Resources in the U.S., 1980–1987." *Economics of Education Review* 11: 19–30.

Zak, P. J., and Knack, S. 2001. "Trust and Growth." *Economic Journal* 111: 295–321.

Zangwill, I. 1994. *The Melting-Pot, Drama in Four Acts*. North Stranton, NH: Ayer. Originally published in 1908.

Zelman et al. v. Simmons-Harris et al., 536 U.S. 639 (2002). ⟨http://laws.findlaw.com/us/000/00-1751.html⟩.

Zimmerman, D. J. 1992. "Regression towards Mediocrity in Economic Status." *American Economic Review* 82: 409–429.

Index